WHY IS EVERYTHING UNDID?

Why Is Everything Undid?

Diary of the first year of divorce

Lana Adams

Copyright © 2023 by Lana Adams.

Library of Congress Control Number:		2023904528
ISBN:	Hardcover	978-1-6698-6122-5
	Softcover	978-1-6698-6121-8
	eBook	978-1-6698-6118-8

All rights reserved. No part of this book may be reproduced or transmitted in any form or by any means, electronic or mechanical, including photocopying, recording, or by any information storage and retrieval system, without permission in writing from the copyright owner.

Any people depicted in stock imagery provided by Getty Images are models, and such images are being used for illustrative purposes only. Certain stock imagery © Getty Images.

Print information available on the last page.

Rev. date: 03/29/2023

To order additional copies of this book, contact:
Xlibris
844-714-8691
www.Xlibris.com
Orders@Xlibris.com

849881

"Mommy, why is everything undid?" my youngest—five at the time—said this one day. She had just disabled an iPad (again), and to pass the fifteen minutes (!), she was playing with a toy we'd had for years—a plastic egg carton with colored eggs where you match the colored shell faces to the inside, but pieces were ALWAYS missing. Three incredible daughters over many years, and I had put that toy back together more times than I could count.[1]

Well, this time we didn't find all the pieces, and my youngest went into full meltdown mode. I had a very clear moment. Her question summed up how I'd been feeling for a very long time—even her

---

[1] I could buy it again for $12.99 on Amazon, and it'll be here tomorrow, but let me enjoy the brain damage of finding all the pieces and putting it back together again and again. I swear the Indiana hillbilly in me gets a high when I find the pieces and don't have to buy a new one. But the high wears off as I'll do it all over again tomorrow or maybe even yet again today. Yay!

improper use of the word "did." Things are *undid* everywhere. They aren't in alignment. Everything needs to be undid and undone. This, paired with pandemic upheaval and a marriage on life support, pushed me to undo the things in my life that felt misaligned with who I truly am.

May

Sunday, May 2

I can't believe I did it. I left my marriage. I'm sitting in my new high-rise apartment. The first apartment I've ever rented myself—a fortysomething white woman with three daughters. Just mine. Paying the rent: me! Fixing the lights: me! Keeping it not disgusting: me! Kids will certainly help (lol, right? RIGHT?). I am so lucky I kept working after having babies as there's no way I could have done this without money in the bank.

I grabbed things quickly and the girls are with me. They think we're on vacation. This doesn't feel like a vacation. I'm so panicky. I took them to the indoor pool in my building and had a cocktail in a Yeti while semi-lifeguarding. My girls can swim on their own (ages twelve, nine, and six) and not having to wear floaties and me not freezing in the pool with them is glorious, but I'm in survival mode. I need to be strong. I can't believe I'm here. Now what?

Monday, May 3

The windows here. The light. I always thought about an apartment with a city view. The town house I lived in was difficult to actually *live* in day-to-day. I've hated it for years, but I wasn't sure if it was the structure of the home or the life in it. I don't have to climb two flights of stairs if my kids forget socks in the morning so that's a positive. And with three daughters, forgetting things happens all the damn time.

Oh, the town house. Chicago's real estate mirage. In 2012 when my middle daughter was born, the town house was all I wanted. I felt like it was the next logical step. We had a loft apartment where the walls didn't go all the way to the ceiling. It was what we could afford at the time, but it was horrible with our firstborn—she cried and wanted to be held nonstop. Even twelve years later, she's sensitive and needs a lot of hugs. The town house was the move every Chicago parent made if they were going to stay downtown. I loved the town house originally and pushed to buy it, but after living there for ten years, it was physically killing me.

Townhomes are multilevel floors of endless stairs and provide so many nooks and crannies that everyone can spread out, but it doesn't feel like a home. It felt overwhelming. I was always all the way up on the fourth floor in the master bedroom with a kid or two, living room and kitchen on the other floors, and then the random "bonus" room on the first floor with coats, shoes, scarves, book bags, workout equipment, and more stuff we didn't need. The stuff was everywhere, and it was impossible to keep it all in the right place.

I hadn't thought much about having a place with more sunlight and a view, but this new apartment is giving me something to think about. So much light and the view is gorgeous—and not only that, but I'm also able to think better. I see things from a higher level, and I don't get as lost in the minutia (speaking more about work, as my girls are "all" minutia).

The town house had no view and barely any light at all. I've got this furnished apartment for a year if I need it, but hopefully, I will figure out if I like a high-rise or not quickly. Looking out the windows is by far my favorite activity.

There's a rental building next to mine, and I can see right in the windows. So far, I've seen a guy go behind a curtain to snap a dick pic down his pants (and a woman was in the living room on the other side of the curtain, watching TV; I assume dick pic was not for her). I've also seen a couple bang on a dishwasher, and I took note of the brand. Seemed sturdy. I've missed this people-watching! I forgot people did stuff like this, as I've spent over a decade in a town house watching Bravo.

Maybe this is the honeymoon phase and I'll hate the doorman nosiness or the parking garage[2] but so far, I'm a fan of the high-rise. My girls like it too.

---

[2] It does take a solid three more minutes to get the kids to school going round and round the parking garage to my assigned parking spot underground. The kids and I call it the City of Embers down there, and I have a whole voice with it. The lights flicker and everything.

Tuesday, May 4

I've never understood the phrase "the silence is deafening." I've been busy my whole life. Between raising a family, getting a master's degree, and a big job, I don't know if I heard real silence before today. I had to take the kids over to the town house to be with their dad. I dropped them off in the home I lived in days before, but I wasn't living there anymore. It was so hard to say goodbye and look at their faces. Confusion still.

I drove the few miles to my new home alone. I felt my throat get tight and eyes watery while I was saying goodbye. I know in my heart this is best for all of us. I shut the car door and started driving, with tears spilling down my face. After getting home I put my purse down and looked around. Nothing but quiet. The toys and wet towels were still on the floor from the kids getting ready earlier. The silence was truly hurting my ears. My therapist says to sit with the uncomfortable, and divorce is a whole new set of uncomfortable and painful moments. Sit in your silence and get comfortable being uncomfortable. I sat in silence and cried for hours. I did not drink, which oddly I'm proud of.

Friday, May 7

I do not want to call my soon-to-be ex-husband my "ex." There's something so negative about "ex," and it diminishes his place as their dad. Yes, we are no longer romantically together, but I believe we can be friends. I hope we can anyway. We were loyal to each other, but after two decades together, we were different people on different paths. We were kids fresh out of college when we got together. We grew apart, and I'm coming to terms with that in therapy.

I'm going to call him my kids' dad (KD for short) instead of ex, so people don't say ex around my kids.

I'll always remember the pain in his eyes when I was leaving. He'd threatened the D word so many times. He didn't want to be the bad guy. I can be the bad guy for him. I know we will be happier this way but, fuck, it's hard dismantling a life that, on the surface, looked perfect.

Sunday, May 2

How do you start telling people you moved out and are getting a divorce when you were seemingly the perfect couple and there is no big reveal—no affair, no big lie, no giant money or gambling problem? And during a pandemic on Zoom meetings where your background went from one home one day to a different home the next day? I guess I could blur out my background, but that messes with me while I present like I'm a shape-shifter melting into the matrix.

Oh, but KD and I looked like the perfect couple. Dual income, high earners, gorgeous kids, and all the "look at my beautiful family" holiday cards you can count. But we weren't happy. The pandemic magnified that—being around each other day in and day out, stressful jobs, and just a general reckoning of "how did we get here?" It accelerated what was already under the surface.

The big new job I got earlier this year also showed me I'm capable of big things. I can't be a leader at work talking transparency in the food industry (my dream job!) when I can't be honest with myself. It would be easier to stay but I just knew in my heart it wasn't right. KD knew it too, but he never wanted to be the bad guy but had no issues throwing the D word around while I made lunches or whatever time of day if he was stressed or irritated about something.

So now comes the fallout. I told sister first. Then my parents and other siblings. And, fuck, were they shocked. Well, sister wasn't, as she knows me better than anyone. My dad. Listening to my dad brought me to tears a few times. He loves me, but he's worried I'm not going to be okay. I didn't have the heart to say I'm worried about that too.

And the weird shit after. The removing of KD from the "my side of the family" group text. These are things I didn't think about. KD cares about optics—what people are saying about him, what's happening that he's not aware of, etc. One of the first things he said when I told him I wanted a divorce was that this would ruin his professional brand. It sounds absurd, but divorce is a very public failure and I feel tremendous guilt about that. KD's career is important to him and he's very good at what he does. I will support him in however he wants to share or talk about this. Is conscious uncoupling still a thing?

I hate that removing him from the 'my side of the family' group text takes something from him. It's bullshit political memes and random movie quotes, but KD's FOMO is real. And his family isn't big, loud, and aren't texting fools like mine.

Maybe when things get better and the shock wears off, we can be some weird, dysfunctional divorced-but-still-on-family-group-texts-together type family—put his new wife on it if he marries again? Writing that doesn't faze me. I want him to be happy. I KNOW. That sounds like crazy talk, but when I think about my future, I'm not sure I want to be attached to anyone ever again. I spent more than two decades this way and I want to undo, unwind, and realign with who I truly am and what I want—not only for me but to show my girls that happiness looks different for some families and that's okay. My inner core just feels off and it has for some time. I can't keep living with something inside that is telling me it needs fixing. I need to get raw, real, and address whatever it is, warts and all.

Wednesday, May 5

The fallout from telling friends and family you're getting a divorce is different, depending on where the person is in their own marriage. For my friends, those that are unhappy in their marriages (like 7/10 of them), their response was "Now you can bang for sport!" and "You should go on a vacation alone! Meet a man in Europe! *Eat, Pray, Love* style."

It's like when someone tells you to clean. You might have the whole afternoon off, but if you don't want to clean that day, you don't want to clean. Sure, I have some newfound free time and I could do anything with it. Cooking class! Painting! Work on myself! But all I feel like doing is thinking and reading so I do divorce correctly and don't mess up my girls too much. Maybe I'll get there, but nothing in me wants to go outside and talk to people. Being around my girls every day all day and then suddenly having time away from them is absolutely excruciating. And I know excruciating pain—our middle girl showed up a week early and I damn near had her in the lobby of Northwestern Hospital sans drugs or any of the good stuff. It was hell. Being away from my daughters is even worse, though.

I went to a restaurant with a few mom friends for Cinco de Mayo. I had to really push myself to get up, get dressed, and go. While I always enjoy seeing my friends, something about this time was different. They were all ranting about their husbands (like usual), but I looked around at all the strangers and wondered how happy they were. If they were on a date. If they were married. It made me really sink down into my own feelings about it. Do I want to go home to someone after this? Do I even care? The solitude hurts, but I want to feel calm and at peace with myself before sharing my life or home again with someone (if I ever do).

I'll try not to be hard on myself and just take my time figuring myself out. Everybody is all "It's summertime in the city!" and "The world is your oyster," and I feel like the world is my toilet.

Sunday, May 9

My first Mother's Day in an upside-down world. I had my kids and saw KD. We are co-parenting but it just feels sad. I know this is the right path for our family. Deep down I know this in the depths of my soul, but often what's right isn't easy.

KD wrote me a card for Mother's Day. I can't open it. Not because I want the marriage back, but not all our marriage was our romantic relationship. It was me as a mother too. The divorce feels like a ding against me as a mom. Like I failed. I know this rationally is not true, but I still feel that way. I can't sit in the uncomfortable of whatever that card says right now.

Tuesday, May 11

Oy. Big job doesn't know I'm divorcing. I just started this new job a few months ago, but when I started on Zoom, my background was different—now it's a high-rise apartment so the jig is up.

There is such a stigma on divorced people. It's like clickbait. What happened to her? He leaves, cheats, she cheats, did they both cheat? Drinking problem? Everyone wants the smoking gun. But there wasn't a smoking gun.

I'm telling people one-on-one when it makes sense. I remember telling coworkers one-on-one when I got engaged a million years ago. I loved my tiny diamond in a cathedral setting. I never wanted an expensive ring or a big wedding. I wanted something simple.

I still love the simplicity of the ring, but when I look at it now, it seems dated. I took it off the day I moved out. I put it in a glass jar with a promise ring KD gave me after a few years of dating. I put the jar away so I couldn't see it every day. I'll get that ring out again someday and do something special with it for my girls.

Telling the engagement story over and over was mildly irritating. Telling your coworkers you're getting a divorce and having to tell it over and over again on awkward Zoom meetings is fucking major irritation, like raw, chafed breastfeeding nips while racking yourself on a bike seat. (Ladies, you know what I mean.)

Could I have picked a worse time to get divorced? All pandemic virtual BS. Yet another thing I didn't think through, but here I am. It doesn't help that I'm awkward and I make inappropriate jokes to make things feel less heavy. But I had no jokes. No fun quips. I'm an emotional person, so every time I got the question (usually benign enough of "Did you guys move?"), I would answer. My throat would get tight and my eyes would well up. I'd quickly shift to the ol' Richard from Friends "I'm okay" head bob. Inside, I'm an anxious mess. It's a relief to say it out loud as I'm finally being honest even if the perfect couple image is shattered.

Thursday, May 13

I want to delete all social media. My Instagram and Facebook are just giant reminders of a life that has been completely blown up. The memories that pop up hit at odd times. My oldest did something to my phone where you see a photo montage as an app icon and I'm too tech illiterate to change it. Every time I look at my phone, I see something that triggers memories of the life I had. While I know this is the right decision, it feels very hard.

Photos from the start of summer a year ago with smiling, sticky faces, Fourth of July together, our beach house memories, first day of school pictures. I took all social media off my phone. Is this going against the therapist's advice of getting comfortable in the uncomfortable? But, fuck, why do I need to get comfortable in something as uncomfortable and inhumane as social media? I'm hanging on by a thread so I think the therapist will understand.

Saturday, May 15

As we go through mediation, our "stuff" is still connected. Been a few weeks now living separately, but our bank accounts, Spotify,

Netflix, and every other app is still shared. I don't need KD to know I watched *365 Days* again on Netflix. It's basically kidnapper porn, although not a kid that gets napped; a woman gets railed. There's a six- to seven-minute boat scene where they have sex for the first time in a bunk, on the deck, over the railing. Truly RAILED. After thinking I was asexual and just not that into sex for many years (forties, drained, big job, kids), turns out, NOPE. The movie perked me right up the first time I watched it. But now I don't even watch the whole movie. I just 'resume watching' and rewind the boat scene. Netflix feels judgey. *Are you still watching this porn, loser?*

I'm not even thinking about men in real life, though, just on the screen so far, but at least I know my lady bits still perk up.

Wednesday, May 19

I've been doing a lot of therapy. It's incredible how little I know myself anymore. Forty-some years in this body and mind, but who the fuck am I? I've busied myself with the wife thing, mom thing, Girl Scout troop leader thing, field trip chaperone thing, career woman thing, but who am I without these things? I don't know yet, but therapy is helping me go through the layers to find out. So many tears, but I always feel better after.

Monday, May 24

Apparently, I have some unresolved trauma. I don't like using that word. I reserve that word for people that have been through much worse. I diminish my pain. I'm not sure why. I talk to sister every day, often multiple times a day. She helps me make sense of it all. I cry daily, and then feel bad for putting all of my shit on her when she's got kids, a big job, and a marriage so I try not to monopolize the conversation, but I know I do.

I do love the light and windows. Every week I feel better here.

Wednesday, May 26

I run a lot. It gives me peace and clarity. I'm always up before the sun rises—been a morning person my whole life. I didn't use to cry during runs. Sometimes, but not often. Now that's all I do. I listen to songs and I just feel all my feelings. I have daughters so we're big on Disney movies. One of the songs I've been listening to on repeat is Phil Collins's "You'll be in my Heart" from *Tarzan*. Ironically, when I hear this song I'm not thinking about KD, marriage, or my own children. I cry because I think about myself. The little girl in me that grew up to a fortysomething woman in desperate need of her own mothering. I'm hard on myself. I don't give myself the same love and kindness that I give to everyone else. When I hear the song, I see grownup motherly me talking to scared little girl me—in the same way I speak to my own daughters. The little girl in me needs the same kindness, strength, and protection from my own mind, and I need to reframe how hard I am on her.

Come stop your crying
It will be alright
Just take my hand
Hold it tight
I will protect you
From all around you

I will be here
Don't you cry.
For one so small
You seem so strong
My arms will hold you
Keep you safe and warm
This bond between us
Can't be broken
I will be here don't you cry.

And I will be here for her. I will be here for her more than I ever have. Just as my girls are my number one priority, so too should the little girl inside me matter. When I hear this song, I cry. Every single time. But I also feel better.

Friday, May 28

My mom did not talk to me about sex, my body, or any of that. She raised me, sure, but doesn't have much of a relationship with me as an adult and doesn't really know my girls. I was woefully unprepared for college and boyfriends, my body, sex, and everything in between. Same with sister.

I didn't have much sex before I got with KD. Like many Gen X women, I was in a self-inflicted pressure cooker in my twenties—get married soon or you'll be too old and nobody will want you. I grew up watching *Sex in the City*, the lobster episode in *Friends*, and other tropey shows about how women are supposed to pair up or be doomed to never find your soulmate or have kids.

I remember pushing KD to get engaged and worrying I wouldn't be able to have kids. I was a perfectly healthy twenty-six-year-old. What in the actual fuck? How many now fortysomething women after years of self-inflicted pressure to lock it down are now divorced or miserably married? If I weren't so tired, I'd look that up. I bet it's a lot. The world seems different now.

While men have always seemed to marry in whatever decade they choose without much fanfare, women need to get engaged in their twenties, married, and all their kids before thirty-five or you are the dreaded advanced maternal age. (I still remember the moment I read 'AMA' on my OBGYN file with my third—RUDE) Countless times I'd sit at bars with girlfriends, and we'd go back and forth on timelines. So many situations like this:

> *Female is dating someone they weren't sure about (and he likely wasn't sure, either), but finding another boyfriend and turning that into a relationship → talking at least a few months to find said boyfriend + one to three years dating + engagement + wedding = damn it, I'll be thirty-five before I even start trying to have kids, and then I'll be responsible for whatever genetic thing I give them with my old eggs.*

Now I have the years behind me to know it's all fine, no matter the path. It didn't feel that way to me in my twenties. I just felt pressure to get to some arbitrary finish line but I'm unclear what that was—locking down a man with a ring? YOU DID IT! YOU ARE NOT THE OLD MAID! But now I'm in old maid category again, I guess?

I would never change anything about my life as it produced three wonderful humans that make my life worth living. I also truly love their dad. He is a good human and the best father. Marriage is more than friendship, though. I wish I had found myself a bit more before getting married. I also should have unraveled my sexual trauma and understood my body and dealt with the shame, guilt, and the negative talk track in my head, but I was in a great big hurry for what, I'm not sure?

Saturday, May 29

I do not have my girls and it's Memorial Day weekend. I'm headed to see my sister, my brothers, and parents. This is the first time I'm seeing my family since telling them the news. KD won't be with me, my kids won't be with me, and I need to drive myself. I don't like to drive. I got a D in driver's ed. For real. So many things I'm learning to do on my own. Part of it is invigorating, but it is scary AF.

So, I'm here at sister's. We went to brother's pool and all the cousins played. But my kids—my part—of the cousins weren't there. It broke my heart. I cried off and on. I didn't cry in front of anyone but sister. She knows my soul. I thank God for her. My mom and dad are being supportive, but I see the worry and "You're making a mistake" look on their faces. My mom is especially colorful with her words: I'm doing life wrong. You have no idea what you are doing. Suck it up, buttercup.

Watching all the cousins eat popsicles and play with pool noodles was both gut-wrenching and comforting. Therapy has been teaching me to work on myself and be the best version of me. Through the sadness, I need to see the positive side too. While I ate and drank too much vodka (bad) and missed my kids terribly (very bad), I was also able to spend time with my nieces and nephews and really talk to them. I hadn't realized how little I had done that over the years, as whenever my kids and KD were at family events, I was dripping in my own kids asking for things.

JUNE

Tuesday, June 1

The doormen at the high-rise flirt with me. I don't recall men flirting with me when I was married. Sometimes, I suppose, but I was more oblivious then. Now I see it and it makes me smile, especially when the old black guy, Frank, is working. He perks me up every time just by telling me I'm pretty and remembering something about my kids. But some days I'm not having it. I flip between feeling very *How Stella Got Her Groove Back,* and then other days I'm *Misery.* You just never know who you'll meet in the hallway that day. But, damn, do I notice the black men around me.

I've been reading a lot. Stages of grief stuff. The emotional intensity of divorce is supposed to peak within the first six months of separation. The whole grieving process may take as long as two years, though. I need to buckle up. This isn't some test I can study for and get an A.

Wednesday, June 2

I'm a white Gen X woman. Silent sufferer. I grew up in a home with far too many kids (four under five, including twins) and parents that struggled—money, marriage, relocation, lack of college education, way too many animals in the house. My mom is tough as nails. She is not an emotional person at all. She said "Shut up" and "Quit your crying" so many times these are go-to voiceovers in my head when I'm faced with my girls whining. I hear them in my head and work so hard to STOP and not say them to my girls. I do not want to diminish their emotions. I want to help them sort through it all and be okay.

I've always been a ball of sensitive. As I've done my own therapy, I've realized so many patterns. My emotional needs have not been met, especially as a child. My physical needs were, but the lack of emotional support led me to anxious attachment style as an adult. I bury my own emotions, I don't ask for help, I judge myself harshly, feel guilt and shame about my own needs, strive for perfection, very sensitive to rejections, apologize constantly, and I'm easily overwhelmed. A whole melting pot of personality traits I manage daily to be a functioning human but, most importantly, a cycle I want to break to be the best mom to my girls.

I've done the psychotherapy, the mindfulness, and meditation. The latest is EMDR which is one of the coolest approaches I've seen for dealing with trauma. In addition to not having my emotional needs met as a child, I've also experienced sexual assault.

EMDR enabled me to unravel troubling memories and beliefs I have connected to them ("I am not good enough") and revise my internal talk track to one of love and positive beliefs about who I am. I've been able to process hurtful memories and fully resolve them and be at peace with myself. Remarkably, most is about treating myself as that inner little girl and giving her grace and kindness. I practice this daily now.

Thursday, June 3

Mediation is going well. I'm surprised. I know KD has been dating, as mom friends have seen him out. He's on dating apps. This doesn't bother me as I truly want him to be happy. My mom friends do not understand this. I will always care for him as the father of my girls, but I do not want to be intimate with him.

It's hard to explain but I have a life vision of happy kids, happy KD with someone else . . . he's a great person so she would be great, too, and I get my happy too. Prob very Pollyanna of me but a girl can dream. I don't know what "my happy" is, though.

He wants fifty-fifty in the agreement with no spousal support. We both have big jobs so that makes sense to me. We are splitting our finances fifty-fifty and the kids fifty-fifty, but I don't think he'll be able to do his fifty percent with the kids all the time. He's always traveling for work. Always at a work dinner. He seems to prefer that over being home.

I travel, too, but like most women, we bang it out. We fly to New York and back in a day. I've done this more times than I can count. Men seem to fly out Sun, leave Wed or Thurs to come back. They do drinks, happy hours, and dinners, plus all the meetings and socializing. I figure out what I need to do and get it done in the tightest timeframe possible and get home because I'm a wreck without my girls. And I dragged a beat-up old Medela breast pump (the pump in style! A horrid looking "purse") all over the country—pumping at LaGuardia, the bathrooms of corporate offices, the back of a car service, on a plane, in the bathrooms at food company headquarters. I'm past those breastfeeding years, but I still get a tingly weird feeling sometimes in the nips thinking I'm engorged somehow even after weaning my last (on her fifth birthday, no less . . . we are crunchy like that).

Saturday, June 5

I hate weekends I don't have my kids. I don't know what to do with myself. I get up on Saturday. The sun is shining, and I go downstairs to the gym in my building. I'm on autopilot with working out as I've done my entire adult life. Up early, make bed, work out, and then get to it. But today I don't feel like doing my usual routine.

I met some work friends for brunch. I don't remember day drinking being called brunch when I went out in my twenties. I don't remember eggs with day drinking, though, so perhaps it is a new concept. I got home and I was sad. I remember reading something ages ago that said in your twenties drinking makes you feel vibrant and alive, but in your thirties it makes you feel very old and very tired. In my forties it just makes me sad. It triggers my depression. I had postpartum depression with my first. I have been on an antidepressant since she was eighteen months old and now she's almost a teenager. It helps, but I still have bad days and drinking makes those days even worse. I often think about quitting alcohol entirely as even small amounts make me feel like garbage. Put that on the to-do list.

Monday, June 7

It is so hard. I did a lot when I was married. KD did a lot too, but he always had more stressful, time-consuming work at his actual work. He was always "on a call," (he had a sign for this while holding his mobile—so very irritating), and conquering the business world was very important to him. I had a great career that I loved, too, but my hours were flexible so I could do many of the drop-offs, pick-ups, and Girl Scout troop leader things. Now I do all of it on my own when I have the girls. The parts I don't like that KD used to do: driving, taking out the trash, putting gas in the car, changing air filters, insurance, and tax stuff. I will learn it all, though. KD is being incredibly kind, though, at helping me, and I help him, too, in different ways (definitely try to prep him before he gets the girls so he knows all the things and has quality time with them when they arrive).

I don't get an afternoon nap on the weekends as much anymore, but as hard as it is, I am seeing some positives. I've always loved crafts and now I can do the messiest, glittery, sparkliest slime creations with my girls without worry of KD's distaste for mess. We've been painting and creating art, slime, flubber, resin, and whatever else we come up with. We bake and cook too. Oldest hates recipes and ad-libs, just like her mom. This feels like me.

Thursday, June 10

As part of mediation, KD and I must watch these really old videos on divorce and how to remain a good parent. I watch parts of it, and it makes me sad. Talking poorly about the other parent to the kids.

I resolve to never do this. Putting the kids first has come easy for me so that part I've got down, but the parts about proper co-parent etiquette were helpful. So many more nuances and considerations for your kids that I never considered. The hardest things are what the kids say to me. It breaks my heart I'm not with them every minute that they are awake, but with school and their own lives developing, I know it will be okay.

KD has been incredibly helpful organizing our finances and with mediation. KD always ran our finances. Seeing our financial story together in the first draft of the mediation agreement made me emotional. Seeing it all together. We started with nothing. We were just two kids out of college. The life we built. What we'll lose. It all feels very heavy.

Tuesday, June 15

The hardest part of divorce is not seeing my kids all the time. Dropping them off at school on the days I know I won't be picking them up and KD will have them for a day or two, I get choked up and don't know what to say. I usually say, "I'll pick you up!" or "You have volleyball and I'll get you after practice." And always "I love you." Now I stumble on my words. I say things like "I love you! See you soon." It works with the younger two, but the oldest . . . she is struggling the most with this. It breaks me to see her pain. Yesterday she said she hates she's only with her siblings all the time, which I hadn't thought of. She wants to be with me and KD all the time too. Give me strength. I know she'll be okay.

On the flipside, KD and I are getting more one-on-one time with each girl, as often I'll take one and he'll have two, and we'll do special things with them. We are sharing our parenting responsibilities very well. I think he likes his new life and that makes me happy.

Thursday, June 17

Its Father's Day this weekend. We live in the city but have a small community of families through the kid's school that all live in the neighborhood. It's a tight-knit group. We get together at parks in the neighborhood and let the kids play while the parents obliterate open-container laws. We'll see the group this weekend.

KD and I have been trying to keep things normal and be a united front as we've told our friend group. Nobody needs to choose sides because we can be in the same room just fine. My mom friends don't buy it. It just can't be. You're pretty! He's hot! You're both successful! They badger me with questions—if I'm angry he's dating and are the women younger? The spurned woman vibe is strong with some of them. It's difficult not to get ragey after seeing my friends. Most of my friends are great (especially my dearest crew—Kate, Mary, Jen, and, of course, my sister), but others *really* want to probe. I find those that investigate, judge, or whatever else tend to project their own marriage issues on me. And, my goodness, do they care what I look like, how thin I am, what I eat. Is it care or judgment? Hard to tell sometimes.

Sunday, June 20

We did it. A successful albeit weird feeling Father's Day. We saw neighborhood friends in the park. I could tell people were talking about us. I did my best to act normal but reinforce that we are, in fact, divorcing, I moved out, kids are okay, and please respect our privacy during this difficult time blah blah blah.

KD asked me over to the house after for an early dinner. The house I used to live in when we were a "normal" family. It's incredibly weird to go to a house you lived in as your kids grew from babies to preteens but you no longer live there. A lot of my things are still there. The high-rise is a furnished apartment so I didn't need furniture and such. I've been getting things over time, but it still feels overwhelming to go to the house I used to live in and just eat dinner and sit on the couch. I can't imagine what it's like for KD. This must be tremendously difficult for him day in and day out there, but we don't talk about that. We keep it focused on the kids.

KD has taken pictures down and got some man candles. The man candle smell is really strong there now. Like a sage lumberjack cashmere woodsman kick to the face when you open the front door. I roll with it. He makes steaks and he looks happy. I get to hang with the kids. Things feel good until I have to leave and the kids stay at KD's for the night. They did not want me to leave. They pull at me. I willed myself to hug goodbye, walked to my car, and cried all the way home.

The number of times I've walked down the street with tears streaming down my face this year—we're talking absurd levels here. People don't notice which oddly makes me happy and more comfortable with my sadness. Nobody is really paying attention.

Monday, June 21

Therapy is getting a little out there. I've been going for some time now and often topics of "I'm not good enough" come up and why I beat myself up so much. I'm a negative thinker with an anxious attachment style, or so she says. It makes sense.

Sex and intimacy come up. I cry randomly. It won't stop, and I just talk and talk and talk. I had a moment where I finally saw me—little girl me. Barely graduated from college, working in a law firm, being sexually targeted, and getting robbed on a train platform coming home from work. A few months later, I met KD. I had never processed nor healed from this trauma months prior, and sitting in my therapy session, I realized my lady bits are also feeling "not good enough."

My therapist loves to give me fun homework assignments. This one was hilarious. Listen to a powerful song while you massage yourself (anywhere you want) and feel your power. No shame, no judgment, it just *is*. I laughed all the way home, thinking I'd never get through this.

Oh, but I did, and it was exceptional. Highly recommend.

Of course, I picked Pat Benatar's *All Fired Up*. I liked the visual of firing up my power—lady bits and all. I did this with a Theragun massager with headphones and later with a vibrator. Both were quite empowering, and Pat Benatar's feminist tough voice just gets you feeling the vibes.

> *All fired up (now I believe there comes a time)*
> *All fired up (when everything just falls in line)*
> *All fired up (we live and learn from our mistakes)*
> *All fired up, fired up, fired up (the deepest cuts are healed by faith).*

Tuesday, June 22

While my time alone is still a little mopey, the time with my kids is fun. The high-rise is furnished, but it's minimal without all the toys and crap that still need to be sorted at KD's. The town house has so many mini levels, and I was always in charge of decluttering the kids' toys and all their crap. It was a lot—hard to get to all of it with those stairs and I'm tired.

He's been packing boxes, and I've been grabbing things. The kids' stuff multiplies like gremlins. At KD's house, the man candle smell greets me every time. He has the same exact scent in his car. You can't get away from it.

I see the sky and so much sunlight in the new high-rise. The kids are settling in. It doesn't feel like vacation anymore, but we do have fun. We play more games. I bought a $3 Old Maid card game at the Target dollar bins. I've revamped how you win. You want the Old Maid. She is fine. She is wise. She is motherly. She is good. Don't ever be afraid of that card.

Thursday, June 24

I had a breakfast meeting for work today. The founder of my company is still heavily involved in the business. I adore him. It's awkward, though, as the word is getting out that I'm getting divorced. He wants to be supportive—most people do—but it's just not something I want to talk about with many people. The pandemic seems to blend work and life so much. Apparently, it's rare for the mom to leave the family home. I had to get out of that house with those stairs. I am going to look for high-rise apartments to buy later this fall, and I want something close to the town house so my girls feel connected. I just wanted to see if I liked it and I really, really do.

Wednesday, June 30

Oy. I don't like doing all the things by myself. Buying a new dishwasher—why are there so many? And what was that brand I saw when that guy was banging that girl on one in the apartment building across from me?

Changing light bulbs, clogged drains and toilets, and fixing drawers that are off the track. I got my work computer all set up and that was a BIG deal for my brain. I have a car and it has so many bits, bobs, lights, and lasers. It always has some sort of exclamation point telling me something isn't right, check engine, oil, doors, ALL of it. Check it now! I have exclamation points all over my life right now. CAUTION! SHIT IS FUCKED UP!

I didn't realize all the things KD handled, and he likely didn't realize all the things I handled. He was better at the house stuff. I'm better at taking care of kids—painting, crafts, playdates, dealing with their friendships, and doctor's appointments. We had very traditional gender roles in the marriage. Now I'm doing it all, and so is he. I always feel like I'm missing something or doing it wrong. I'll figure it out. What is "it" exactly, I'm not sure? KD has been great at helping me. I am so glad we can be amicable. I have dreams we can still be a family, albeit a nontraditional one.

July

Thursday, July 1

I'm down today. I have the girls today, but KD has them for the weekend. It's the first big holiday when I'll be alone. It's so hard to go from being a mom doing things with your family every holiday to being alone. I have friends and I try to get out and do things, but often it's drinking or brunch (makes me sad), or being with mom friends and their kids, which also makes me sad as my kids aren't there. So here I sit in purgatory, trying to figure out what I'm going to do with my free time this weekend without my kids. Is it always going to be this hard? I get choked up thinking about it. I keep taking sleeping pills and I know I shouldn't, but I just want the day to end so I get to the next day when I'll see my kids.

Saturday, July 3

I'm trying to *Eat, Pray, Love* it out this weekend alone. I don't travel alone but a staycation *Eat, Pray, Love* sounds right up my alley. I went to a painting class today. I love to paint but I don't know the proper technique. We recreated a painting of a woman with a giant afro, and the afro became the sun and sky. I did my version of it with lots of yellow (my favorite!) and blue. I loved what I made. She's very Sasha Fierce. I don't feel like her yet, but I know she's in me.

Tuesday, July 6

Made it through the holiday weekend. I had my therapy appointment earlier. I'm getting tired of talking trauma and "not good enough." I still feel like trauma should be reserved for people with *real* trauma (I'm not sure what real trauma is but my mind goes to the really bad stuff—someone tried to kill you, terminal illness, you had a child die (this would end me I'm sure of it), you had family members die unexpectedly, etc. OMG, I'm not good enough to use the word trauma to describe my own experience. Ain't that some ironic shit?

I tell my therapist things—getting mugged, getting taken advantage of sexually without consent, and just general "I'm not good enough" stuff. Remarkable how resilient I am, but I bury my feelings and don't address them. When I speak about parts of my life—especially intimate parts—I cry. When I talk about sex, I immediately feel bad. Bad that I didn't have it often enough with KD. Bad that I didn't want to. Bad that I don't know my own body. I have a negative talk track inside that I need to unwind and rewire. I'm going to keep peeling all those layers back to see what's underneath, no matter how upsetting.

Wednesday, July 7

Every day feels like upside-down world. I'm trying to dress professionally for work (have to go in now one to two days a week, especially when the founder visits). I wear dresses as I fancy myself like Steve Jobs and his turtlenecks. It's easier to pick one thing versus trying to match a top and bottom. I get compliments a lot, but when I do, I feel like a fraud. It's easy to put a dress on, heels, and some lipstick. It masks all the sadness and pain on the inside. I have a great body for a fortysomething and put a dress on it and I look pulled together. But underneath I'm falling apart.

Thursday, July 8

I have a hard time being the person who initiated the divorce. KD threatened it many times over the years but did not do it. I don't like when people ask or infer that my husband left me, but I also don't want to immediately scream back "I LEFT HIM!" like I'm the winner here. Nobody is the winner here. There's so much pain on both sides. Trying to claim a winner is absurd.

Saturday, July 10

I took the kids over to the beach house KD and I have owned together for years. It's across the street from Lake Michigan and has a golf cart and a fun neighborhood for the kids to play in. I haven't gone here alone yet. The beach house is so quiet. The kids play like usual, but everything around the house reminds me of the life I used to have. I know this is the right thing but it feels overwhelming. I started panicking after looking around the house. We're talking about KD keeping the town house, and I take the beach house and then I buy a condo in the city. While I'm incredibly proud I can afford two homes on my own, thinking about maintaining them freaks me the fuck out. The beach house is a little over an hour away from where I live in the city and seeing it—really looking at the house and all the things I'll need to do to keep it intact—hit me. The landscaping, wood pile, the golf cart battery (that thing is so heavy!), the loose porch railings. How am I going to do this? Sister is willing to help me; she even got a handyman to come over and organize the wood pile and power wash the porch, but I am overwhelmed thinking about how I'll do it all.

My therapist gave me a Xanax prescription. I only take it when I'm panicking and can't calm down. When I take it, I fall asleep within forty-five minutes, and then I find it difficult to smile or show much emotion for a few days. I took it on a Sunday once and didn't smile until Wednesday.

I suppose it helps in the moment, but the aftermath sucks—I don't want to be panicky, but I don't want to be an emotionless bot, either. Is taking a Xanax better than just downing a bottle of wine or a few sleeping pills? I'm not sure.

Saturday, July 10

I'm still over at the beach house. So overwhelming to think this five-bedroom house will be mine after the divorce. I tend to play an anxiety game with myself. How many dark, overwhelming thoughts can I think about in one sitting? Therapy tells me to focus on what's in front of me and try not to get too lost in future worries. I suck at doing that when I'm alone.

I'm sitting on my screened-in porch alone, listening to the rain. I'm calm but so, so sad. I don't want to be with KD romantically and coming to terms with that is really upsetting. I always think there's something wrong with me. That I'm incapable of feeling the way I'm supposed to feel, and if I'm honest about the way I truly feel, I will hurt someone. So, I keep things in and put a smile on my face, but life is too short to be unhappy. I know this. KD deserves a wife that wants to be with him in all facets of what a wife should be. I'm not sure I'm capable of that. Sex. The big SEX word. I have always thought of myself as not very sexual. Could go weeks or months without it and be fine, but that's not what KD wants nor expects (nor should he). I'm a feeler, though, and words, threats of divorce, and whatever else have impacted me over the years.

Wednesday, July 14

Man, the camps and kid activities are hard to manage while divorcing. Every summer we piece the weeks together with Scotch tape and glue sticks, but this year feels tremendously different. Scattered, disorganized. I can't wait for August so school can start again. I need a schedule. Upside-down world feels even more upside down when kids have something at different times every day in two-hour increments, and we divide and conquer on where they go and who gets them there. I've never talked to KD this much! It feels very businessy, and he's been great with it. He seems happy. A lot happier than I am but it's not a contest. I know what I need to do to get my happy. I need to understand me and what I really want. You'd think after forty-plus years I'd know but I lost myself for a long time.

Tuesday, July 20

My mom doesn't call me. It hurts. I know she loves and cares for me but her emotional IQ lacks, especially with me as an adult. It's like she doesn't know what to do if I come to her with any emotion. If I cry, it's "Buck up, quit that crying!" But sometimes (hell, all the time these days) I want to cry. So, I don't call. She doesn't call me, either. Sister is there for me, always. She answers the phone every time I call, and she truly listens. She knows when I need to just cry, and she'll be patient to hear it all. She has her own family, demanding job, and all the things. God gave me her to survive this world. I know this.

Thursday, July 22

One thing I like about getting divorced: I really try to make the moments count with my girls. All the moments are up to me. What I want to do with them (with their input, of course). What we want to eat. What things we watch. I enjoy doing my own thing more than I realized I would. I do feel scared and alone, especially when I don't have the girls, but I try to remember I'm part of this, too, and in a few short years, they will grow up. They'll have their own lives. I see this starting already with my oldest. What will there be for me if I don't find out who I am and what I want? This is pretty much my last shot before I get so tired in my fifties, sixties (God willing, I get there) that I don't make any big moves. It's scary as hell, though.

We are watching all my favorite movies from childhood. *Overboard* (the original, not that awful remake) is my favorite. Seeing my kids watch it and hear their comments—"IT LOOKS SO OLD!"—gives me so much joy. I think about the Kurt Russell character, Dean. I think I want a Dean again someday.

Saturday, July 24

I fluctuate between very kid-focused things when I have the girls to very figure-me-out me-focused things when I don't have them. Today I went to AIRE bath spa. Alone. This was scary. I've never gotten a massage before. I heard AIRE was gorgeous and had salt baths, too, so I booked the 'athlete ritual' and gave it a go. I absolutely loved it. It was uncomfortable to be in the salt baths while couples canoodled around me, but I was Zen after getting a sixty-minute massage. Who knew the Sybaris rebranded to bath spas and now it's classy?

August

Friday, August 6

Movies, massages, music. I have a theme. Sister and brother-in-law came for the Dave Matthews Band concert. Sister has been such a support system for me. She told me I talk about divorce a lot. I know I do. It's an all-consuming topic. I feel guilty I put so much on her. I don't have many people that I can be straight with. She's always been that for me. I hope I do the same for her, but right now I feel like I'm taking up all the air space and it's driving me batty. Will I ever get back to normal?

We walked to the concert, and sister had too much to drink. We walked home, and she was basically bear-hugging me. We are twins. No matter how old we get, if we are together and men are around, we'll get the "threesome" comments. We went to the same college, and it happened there a lot too. What makes men think you'd fuck your sister with them? I have internal comebacks that I never say aloud—"Absolutely! Invite your brother and we'll make it a whole incest foursome TikTok challenge. We're so down. Gotta get dem views."

Back to Dave. I love Dave Matthews Band. So many of his songs speak to me and I can remember where I was when I first heard them. "Pig" is an all-time favorite song.

> *Is this not enough*
> *This blessed sip of life, is it not enough?*
> *Staring down at the ground?*
> *Oh, then complain and pray for more from above*
> *Ya greedy, little pig*
> *Stop, just watch your world trickle away*
> *Oh, it's your problem now*
> *It'll all be dead and gone in a few short years.*
> *Oh, just love will open our eyes*
> *Just love will put the hope back in our minds*
> *Much more than we could ever know*
> *Oh, so, don't burn the day away*
> *Don't burn the day away.*

I do feel like a greedy little pig. Like, what do you want? What would make you happy? I want love around me. I want to feel my power and be intimate again. I have so much work to do to get there. I feel like I'm living in this part of the song right now:

> *Oh, come sister, my brother*
> *Shake up your bones, shake up your feet*
> *I'm saying open up and let the rain come pouring in*
> *Wash out this tired notion*
> *Oh, that the best is yet to come*
> *But, oh, while you're dancing on the ground*
> *Don't think of, oh, when you're gone.*
> *Love (love), love (love), love (love), what more is there?*

'Cause we need the light of love in here
Don't beat your head, dry your eyes
Let the love in there
There's bad times but that's OK
Just look for love in it
And don't burn the day away.

I'm shaking up my bones, my feet, and my whole life. The rain is pouring in. I need to dry my eyes and let love in. Love myself and truly believe I am enough. I don't know where I'd be without therapy. Helps me see so much about myself that I can't see even though I spend all my time with me.

Monday, August 9

I can't wait for the kids to go back to school. I'm ready for routine again. I've also been looking at places to buy. I know I like high-rises, and I want to be close to where KD lives, so I'm searching near there. There's a lovely realtor who has so much style in her pictures. She also lives in a building I adore in the neighborhood. Her name is Iris. Seems like she could be a friend too. We talked a few times, and she's on the hunt for me.

Wednesday, August 11

Work has been such a nice distraction from my divorce. I got this job early this year and I felt empowered. I was sought after for the role, which was a huge ego boost. The first few months were rocky. I swear I was like Brooks in *Shawshank Redemption*. You stay at a company your entire life—more than twenty years—and you get institutionalized. I wanted to stay forever, but once I got to the top and looked around, I realized I could do more. I was so afraid of what another role could look like as the job I had was fine, but something in my gut was telling me to make the move. I couldn't ignore the massive pay bump and size of the opportunity, so I took a leap of faith.

Taking on a big new role was a giant moment of self-reflection. I had felt stagnant for years, but I didn't do anything about it. Making a big career move led me to examine all the things in my life that didn't feel right—the gnawing gut feeling needed to be addressed. It was like being pushed out of a plane. The next thing to tackle was my marriage. I knew this even before I took the job, but it was truly the catalyst that made me realize I have so much left to do on this earth.

I wonder how many women think they can't and so they don't. It's overwhelming to make big changes. Doing them one at a time helped, and the bigger changes propelled me to go even further to fix all the inside turmoil.

I'm a big fan of habit snowball type stuff where small daily habits build up (like a snowball) to a great day, week, month, year, and ultimately life. I wear workout clothes to bed so working out is easier in the morning. I'm religious about getting my fruit and veggies and making my bed. I also took this approach to changing big, big things, and with every new change, I'm inspired to do even more.

Friday, August 13

Every week I'm wanting to tackle something new that feels out of whack in my life. I feel like Cher in *Clueless*. *"Good. Now that takes care of our minds and bodies, but we should do something good for mankind or the planet for a couple of hours."*

The next frontier for me is purely sexual. Not that I want to have sex. I'm not ready for that yet. I am ready to understand why I've felt asexual for my adult life. I've never been all that into it. I don't have much experience and married young. I have three lovely daughters so, of course, sex happened somewhere over the years, but my body (or maybe my mind?) has not desired sex.

It just wasn't something I thought about much over the years. Now on my own, I'm interested in exploring myself and understanding me. I bought a vibrator that actually inserts like a penis! I've only used vibrators on the outside, and often I wouldn't have it touch my skin. I remember seeing veiny gross dildos friends had in my twenties. I was so worried about "hot dog down a hallway" stretched out sitch down there, so I never did that. I liked the small vibrators for outside use only as they somehow seemed safer and not as dirty. But really, what's dirty about one that inserts if you clean it? But why dirty? Oy. Lots to unpack there.

Saturday, August 15

I took the girls over to my friend Mary's pool. My neighborhood group of moms is such an awesome village. Our kids play; the moms cackle and recharge. Everybody wins. I met another school mom at the pool, Kate. She was new to the school and I liked her immediately. She's divorced/widowed and has two kids. I invited her over to my apartment after the pool, and we had an incredibly emotional cry about different aspects of our lives in a span of a few hours. It felt awesome to bond with another mom like that. I can tell Kate is going to be a good friend. It's also nice to know another single mom in the neighborhood.

Tuesday, August 17

Our Zoom divorce meeting is coming up. Apparently, it only takes fifteen minutes. I'm anxious about it. The mediation appointments have been relatively easy, although sad. Seeing KD's face and how 'all business' he is when talking finances, splitting holidays, and the school calendar. He has pulled all the financial materials together and is stoic.

I adore him as a human, but I do not feel romantic feelings for him. I've talked about this over and over in therapy. I don't know what happened, but somewhere along the way, two people grew in different directions. I'm not sure I'm meant to be married, live with someone, and do all of those things. I love being a mom. I love my girls and taking care of them, seeing their personalities, and watching them achieve great things. I did not love the day in and day out of married life. Resentment builds up over many, many years and, ultimately, things felt heavy. KD wasn't happy. I wasn't happy. Everything felt heavy. Living on my own is hard, but it doesn't feel as heavy and I don't feel watched or criticized, but I also don't know if I perceived a lot of those things while married, and maybe I'm the problem? I'm sure I'm part of the problem, but KD threatened divorce so many times it became a broken record, and there's only so many threats you can take.

Thursday, August 19

Kids go back to school soon. Hooray! I need the routine and order again. We've been having fun, but I'm exhausted trying to keep it fun. We've been to the indoor pool in the building so many times. I don't like to swim, but I do get in the hot tub. My kids have a great life. I know I upended it, but in the end, they will be okay. I never got to swim consistently when I was a kid in a gorgeous indoor pool with a hot tub. I'm clearly trying to look on the bright side today. Somehow, they still say "I'm bored," yet we are overlooking the lake in a high-rise in a gorgeous city. Giant eye roll.

Tuesday, August 24

First day back at school. KD and I did the whole thing as a co-parenting unit. The first day back pictures, walk to school, and saying hello to friends we hadn't seen over the summer. It felt right to be together as friends, parents, and two humans that love our tiny humans and seeing them into the building to start a fresh school year. I cried all the way home alone, though. Everything in me does not want to walk back to the town house. I walk in a different direction to my new apartment. This is the way I want to walk, but it doesn't stop the tears and grief for a life I had before when it all made sense even if we weren't happy. I say we because I know he wasn't happy either, and his smile and laugh today was genuine. KD is going to be okay—better than okay—and I love seeing him so happy.

I know it sounds crazy, but I see a partner for me someday; maybe not marriage or a relationship in the traditional sense, but someone that speaks to my soul. I'm a strange, emotional, shy, confident, overanalyzing, quiet extrovert introvert. I have a teenage boy's sense of humor. I don't like most men. Some say that's picky; I say that's a grown, independently successful woman who already had her kids and is choosing a man just *for her*, if she chooses one at all. I do know he's a man. In my asexual journey, I also considered if I was a lesbian. I even watched lesbian porn. I can unequivocally say I am not a lesbian.

September

Wednesday, September 1

The interwebs tell me today is Sock Day. Apparently, a Harry Potter reference where Dobby gets a sock and is freed. Today my divorce was final. Mediation took four months. KD and I were on a circuit county video call in different locations. He was at work. I was in a conference room at work and I had to meet with our CEO right after. I dialed in at the time I was told and when I joined, I heard other people talking and I realized I'm listening to another couple divorcing. It is heartbreaking, somehow funny but also incredibly awkward as I'm in a conference room and had a CEO to meet with right after. I can't be late! Got to get this divorce done.

Our hearing was an hour late. I had no way of knowing who these couples were and where we were in the queue. Then they called our name. It only took twenty minutes. I was emotional. Seeing KD's face. More than twenty years with this human. Deep love for each other, but we both had a realization our path was going to be different. I looked at his face and remembered the good. Only the good. And I thought of our kids. I had to go to the bathroom to take deep breaths and get back to work. In hindsight, I should have taken the day off to process the weight of it, but I always take on too much, thinking I'll be okay.

I went home, sat on my couch, and looked out the window of the high-rise. While I was sad about the end of my marriage (All the legalese say "dissolution of marriage," did it dissolve? Is it bath bomb?), I was also hopeful.

Saturday, September 4

Labor Day Weekend. Sister and I drank too much. As typical three-day weekend holiday summer Saturdays go as now fortysomething moms who drank too much in their twenties: kids get you up early, you have day drinking of some sort set up somewhere—pool, beach, boat, but proper child supervision and fun ensues. We did all that today, but I also made time for lunch with a high school friend who used to write me notes in math class.

He looked so different but the same. I did not feel much romantic chemistry and I knew it immediately. It was so nice to see him, though, and I know we'll be friends as he's divorced too—a few years ahead of me in this shitstorm of a new life. I'm happy I put myself out there.

Saturday night . . .

So I'm riding high on my "putting myself out there" award (self-given) and think, let's be even more courageous. I'd had too much vodka. Sister and I did an online dating profile for me on Tinder, of all things. We picked that one out of all the others as it felt more casual/less eHarmony FIND YOUR SOULMATE TODAY (nope!). As I'm talking to friends though—especially younger females—Tinder is apparently a hookup app, so I may have picked the wrong place to start. Le sigh.

I'm looking for something in the middle between that old eHarmony guy with the glasses spouting soulmate and swipe/bang/leave you faster than Jimmy John's Tinder. BUT here we are.

I hated doing the profile. I don't like talking about myself or selling myself like that. I didn't know what to put and have no idea what I'm looking for or doing with dating, so just said I was recently divorced and "don't know what I need next." I put recent pictures so I wasn't catfishing anyone, and sister reviewed. I opened my app after a few days and it was overwhelming. Not bragging, but I had thousands of likes (swipes? I dunno). I've kept myself in shape and give off MILF vibes IRL, but I think "don't know what I need next" was the wrong thing to add. Many of the initial gentlemen (Who knows, though, could be rats? Catfish?) who reached out said something along the lines of "I know what you need next. Sex. With me." Perhaps I failed out of the gate on the profile.

Monday, September 6

So, on Tinder you have to review likes and then swipe on them too, then you match. I'm still beyond confused with it. I somehow super liked somebody I was trying to reject. This is awful. I'm not focusing on it like I should. I let conversations drift, and then I don't respond. A few are nice so we communicate through the app. One guy said he was a sergeant in the military. His pictures were sexy and he was in his late forties. He said he lived in Chicago, and when I asked where in the city, he said, "Chicago, Illinois." I immediately thought, *Who the fuck talks like that?* I then told the dude I don't believe you and send something that backs up anything he's saying. Yeah, he could not. He did try to photoshop my name on a piece of paper that said, "Hi, Lana" and it was the same photo from his Tinder profile—did he time travel? Think I can't see shit photoshopping skills? This all happened in a week and I feel drained. I'm spending my energy on this?

Wednesday, September 15

Therapy is teaching me to look at things differently. Go for different types of men than I've experienced. Go for what I'm really chemically and physically attracted to. Keep taking the next right step that feels true to me. For now, I'm calling this strategy "what feels right," but it's just gut instinct.

I've been looking at sex differently too. Well, not sex with another human yet, but with myself. Untangling why I feel asexual. The vibrator I bought that inserts is a sleek black. It turned me on the most when I looked at it online and there was something symbolic to buying a black vibrator/wand thing, as it's the first real sex toy I've owned that inserts (like a dick!) and doesn't just stay outside, stimulating the clit. I grew up in the era of 'don't stretch it out down there,' but, meh, now that I've had my kids, I don't care about old tropes. But this sleek black vibrator jumped off the screen. Not just the color black but how it made me feel. I'm a fortysomething-year-old woman who did not know clit orgasms felt different from clit and vagina together. Like levitating. I also didn't know I was capable of having an orgasm that wasn't clit-related. I'm full of surprises!

Saturday, September 18

I like looking at patterns. Things that help me understand myself. In the cesspool that is Tinder, I see my Likes and then those I matched with and it's black. Black, black, black. But it's also different from the traditional white-collar executive types. I'm drawn to different-looking (and working) men: mechanics, military, police officers, firemen, and whatever else tickles my fancy.

The black ones intrigue me the most. Just something about their faces, their skin, their hands, how they carry themselves, the swagger. All the swagger. Pretty sure Eddie Murphy making out with Halle Berry in *Boomerang* on that couch planted the damn seed and it's grown in me for decades but never something I acted on.

Now that I'm free to do 'what feels right,' I'm leaning in the direction of black men as my most arousing/chemistry attraction, hands fucking down. I've been telling sister all about it. She laughs, as I'm sort of racial profiling via online dating app.

Tuesday, September 21

I've been talking to a black man on Tinder. He lives in another state. He's educated. He has charisma. He is kind. We talked for a few days on the app, but I gave him my phone number fast. Then he called me. He called many days after that. We talked about everything. His life, his childhood, his pressures, and divorce. It was nice to listen to someone and feel like they understood. I listen to every word he says too. He's years ahead of me in the divorce aftermath, and I learn something every time I talk to him. I'm going to call him the Ally.

Thursday, September 23

Lord. The Ally makes me do things I haven't normally thought about or done. He's asking me questions about sex, but also life, business, kids, and history, and, damn, he's a genius-level human. But the sex stuff, he is probing on. I'm not going to lie. I'm super type A and have a list on my phone of the things I want to do post-divorce that I felt like were truly me but I hadn't experienced yet. Much of the list was sex things. The Ally is like an investigative journalist about this. It is hard not to be intrigued, but then I feel myself go deep into the feels for him.

With the distance, we're communicating daily, and it gets pretty hot. I'm a mother. Why am I taking pictures of myself? Goofy selfies so he sees my day-to-day life, sharing stupid stories, and just showing myself. All of my damn self. He's still calling, and I love it so, so much. He sends a picture in a pair of pajama pants, and I see the outline of his dick. I am deceased.

Saturday, September 26

I deleted Tinder to focus on the Ally. Someone I have not met. He lives across the country. He says he visits my city often. I try to remind myself, "It hasn't even been a month since you matched with this dude, chill." No man wants the when/where/what female full court press. OMG is it hard not to do it, though. I really like him.

Tuesday, September 29

I moved out months ago and I spent time on myself, and while I loved doing that, I didn't have anyone but sister who I could share things with. A man's perspective is incredibly helpful, and I forgot how much I liked having it. Personal things, life moments, job issues, and support when I'm feeling anxious—the Ally is there for it all. He makes me feel safe.

Safe to talk about my inexperience and failures. Safe to cry and get upset. Safe to hear things about myself I might not like. In talking to him, I realize how defensive I get when I perceive criticism, but when I give myself space to think, I know he's right.

We talk about all the work we've done on ourselves. The therapy and self-reflection. My part in why my marriage didn't work. He also made me feel safe to talk about sex and how I feel about it and why. He calls almost every day. Every time I talk to him, he teaches me something. When he calls, I stop what I'm doing—no matter the time of day—and I pick up. I listen to every word he says completely in the moment and lost in his brilliance and humor.

It makes my heart race every time I see his name pop up on my phone. I'm trying to be "Easy, breezy, beautiful Cover girl," but I am deep in the feels for this human.

October

Saturday, October 2

I'm still loving the high-rise. I am now officially friends with Iris, the gorgeous realtor I met in the neighborhood. She lives in the building I dream about. She's keeping an ear out for me if any units become available. I want a view where I can see the sun rise every day.

Iris is just so stylish. She's from Albania and gives me such positive energy every time I'm around her. I want to dress better and eat better when I'm with her. Call me crazy, but I love friends that are aspirational. She's got a great marriage too and is head over heels for her husband. I love feeling happiness around me, and Iris is like a bottle of stylish optimism.

Tuesday, October 5

I've dressed as a Disney princess every Halloween for many, many years. I started when my oldest was in preschool, and she's almost a teenager now.

I've been them all (well, those that are culturally appropriate for a white woman)—Cinderella, Snow White, Belle, Elsa, Rapunzel, Aurora (Sleeping Beauty, duh), Anna, and this year I'm doing Merida from *Brave*. The costume arrived!

The Merida wig (giant, red unruly curls) gives me White Snake video vibes. I'm a child of the 80s and 90s and Tawny Kitaen was the shit. I am ashamed to admit I snapped a photo and sent it to the Ally. He is both horrified and aroused.

Friday, October 8

It is crazy to have complete control of my finances now. KD had managed our finances our whole marriage. After twenty-plus years now I have an app on my phone with MY accounts! My 401K, my checking and savings account. We have a joint account for child things, and each contributes equally to that, but everything else is mine with my own passwords. I'm continuing to play a "How much money can I save this month?" game where I get paid and move a lot to my savings account. Then I live off cash until I get paid again. When the cash is gone, it's gone. So far, this is keeping me from GrubHub and Uber, and it's giving me a daily momentum jolt to see how far I can stretch a carton of eggs, some greens, salad mix, chicken, and protein powder with fruits/veggies. "This feels right" as I'm an Indiana hillbilly and frugality (and oddly punctuality) are huge for me. These things make me feel peaceful. Sister says the same thing. There's something so satisfying about finishing what's in your fridge and not ordering takeout.

I wish I could play this game all the time but sadly it's more for when I don't have the girls. When I do have my kids, I am often tired and $60 of GrubHub Chick-Fil-A has absolutely been delivered and it comes in a box no bigger than a Happy Meal. $60. HAPPY MEAL SIZE. For nugs.

Wednesday, October 13

The Ally is going to visit. One day, it sounds like. We will do dinner. I am excited, nervous, and all the things. Originally when we matched, I pooh-poohed the idea of talking to someone long distance. I didn't realize he was long distance on Tinder (did he have a giant radius?), but as he started calling almost every day for weeks, I fell into it. The Ally makes me feel sexy like I've never felt before. He tells me he wants me, and it makes me feel like I'm floating.

Monday, October 18

I've been so wrapped up in my feelings for Ally. I'm doing well at my newish job (will be a year in Jan!). I've always been so good at work. I have a specialized role as a dietitian who counsels food and beverage companies on everything, from marketing to ingredient renovations. I can be with the fanciest of the fancy C-suite execs or with plant workers and egg farmers and still do a great job.

Somehow, through twenty-plus years of a career, I still second-guess whether I'm good enough. More to untangle in therapy . . . so many people are like this. You're told in every performance review, you are doing great, exceeding expectations, and get promoted left and right for years. Yet you always feel like the other shoe is going to drop.

Like Viv said, "The bad stuff is easier to believe." *Pretty Woman* was so far ahead of its time. I know this is imposter syndrome, but I have the *actual* goods—a master's degree in my field and I know my shit. QUIT IT, Lana.

Wed, October 20

KD has a girlfriend. He is traveling every weekend he doesn't have the kids. I'm proud of him. He is happy. He has goals, ambition, and he's doing it. He's traveling more now than he ever has. He's spending quality time with the girls because he must. I'm not there to be their crutch or entertainer. On the flipside, when I have the girls, I can be the entertainer, cook, slime maker, painting teacher, or whatever else I want to be. This feels like the rightest right of the whole divorce. Seeing KD happy and traveling the world. Seeing me happy and truly loving myself. I had long considered myself very much broken.

The Ally comes on Friday. We are meeting for dinner, and he has a hotel room. It's so crazy to finally meet someone you've only had a phone relationship with, but we've been talking for what feels like ages. I've never been more excited in my life.

Friday, October 21

I finally met the Ally in real life. He was everything I wanted and a million pounds more. Sexy, funny, sweet, strong, witty, and encouraging.

I've never kissed a black man. Never touched a black man romantically. His smooth skin, his hands, his deep voice. He made me feel safe immediately. We had dinner and, I kid you not, I reached over and lightly touched his leg. I thought I was touching high thigh, but was ~~way too close~~ OKAY, FINE, ON TOP OF his cock, and I could feel it through his pants. I gently rubbed it, and I wanted him more than I could breathe. We went back to his hotel room. I felt safe. I trusted him.

You know those songs you hear growing up that talk that "all night long" shit?

"There were nights of endless pleasure" Celine Dion propaganda. I'm fortysomething and never had a night of endless pleasure EVER. Endless? And a whole night of it? Like eight hours? Yeah, no, Celine. I barely get sleep, let alone nights of endless pleasure.

But I'm not kidding when I tell you I lived that in real life today. The Ally was everything I wanted when I fantasized about black men. But he was so much more than that. He made me laugh until my stomach hurt.

Saturday, October 22

The Ally was only in town for one day. He is older than me but not by much. He has concerns I'm all brand-new to this and need time before starting a relationship. I don't care what we call it, but I need this man in my life in some consistent, real way.

Sunday, October 31

KD and I did a joint Halloween in the neighborhood with our kids. All of our friends were there. It was such a good co-parenting moment. He was happy, and our girls were happy. My Merida from *Brave* costume was a complete bust. Nobody knew who I was. Men were leering at me; perhaps, it was the Tawny Kitaen/girl from White Snake video vibes. If I'm being honest, *Brave* wasn't the best movie—the daughter turns the mom into a fucking bear after a disagreement. I feel this already with my oldest.

Every Halloween since I've been a princess, I carry little glass stones in my gloves—the things you get at craft stores that fill up vases. I call them fairy tears and I give them to children and tell them to keep them, make a wish, and the fairy tears will protect them. I know this is absolute hogwash, but kids' eyes light up when a Disney princess gives them something magical on Halloween. It warms my heart. And it is not candy.

Epic fail on the princess choice this year, though. I still gave out fairy tears and that made me smile. Maybe the Ally has a cosplay fetish, and we can be medieval lovers, or I can just crawl on the hood of his car sometime with the wig on and a pair of ripped stonewashed jeans.

November

Wednesday, November 3

I hate to say it, but things are cooling off with the Ally. We still talk a lot—daily texts, for sure—but not on the phone as often. I got into my feels and probably overshared that too early. I'm trying to dial it back while staying open to the possibility that this won't go anywhere. I'm not sure where I want it to go, though, but my heart wishes for him to say he wants a committed thing with me.

Then the calls are fewer, and I get mad at myself for being so vulnerable. He's got a big job with a ton riding on it—kids and all the things too—and he was very careful and transparent. I knew this was a possibility. It's hard not to take it personally. The old feeling of "Am I not good enough?" rears its ugly head.

He's pulling back and I can feel it. It hurts and I feel out of control. I know I need to continue working on myself and truly be happy being alone. And I was before I met him. Why did I do this to myself?

Sunday, November 13

Thanksgiving is next week. This is a holiday where KD, the kids, and I would either go to my family or to his. This year we're doing a joint thing at the town house.

I still talk to Ally, but not nearly as frequent. I'm working through my feelings about it. I spent the last two-plus decades with one man, and we had grown so far apart I was thinking I was asexual. Now I'm out in this world and I've had all these revelations about myself in a short time frame . . .

You are not asexual.

You love sex.

You are a sensual woman, like off the charts passionate emotive person, and

Energy and chemistry are crucial.

But meeting Ally took these revelations (mainly gleaned from therapy) and put them in real life as the truthiest truths of my life.

I know my intensity pushes him away. I feel like a raw, exposed nerve around him and not because I need to sit in some arbitrary waiting room to be ready to be with someone again. Realizing these things about myself forced open a locked basement I didn't know I had. Opening that door—opening myself up to someone, being vulnerable with my most private thoughts, opening my body up to pleasure, and truly being in the moment—I was basically spilling over with constant emotion and it's too much. I am too much.

Friday, November 19

Every day I get up and immediately look at my phone to see if the Ally has texted. Most days now, it's no. Le sigh. He has his own issues and a lot he's dealing with personally. I am trying to understand and be there for him as a friend or whatever we are. I've never been good at playing it cool. I have confidence and know I'm pretty dang awesome, but I say what I feel. I should zip it sometimes, though.

Wednesday, November 24

OMG, today sucks. I'm in bed. I have the day off. It is Thanksgiving tomorrow. I do not have my kids today. I am listless. The sky is gray. It is cold. I am not motivated to do anything. I decided to tackle something I've been putting off for months so it can (hopefully) catapult me back to get shit done mode. I get up and wear my favorite athleisure to the DMV to renew my driver's license.

A lovely man chats me up while waiting in line FOR AN HOUR. I can only see that he is black and tall. He has a mask on, a winter hat, and coat. Hard to see what this man really looks like, but I enjoy talking to him. He gave me his card. It's a nice feeling to be out and about in the world and have someone notice you.

Thursday, November 25

KD and I hosted Thanksgiving together at his town house. KD was always good at entertaining. He loves an IPA and grilling out. He makes steaks, and we have loads of sides and appetizers. The girls and I make a dessert table. We enjoy the time together as a nontraditional family. I'm feeling good about that part of my life. I know the kids are resilient, and they just need love. They need to see and feel love around them. I'm trying to do that every day and know KD is too.

It's nice to see him so happy and he's opening up about his girlfriend and concerns about settling down too fast with one of the first women he connected with on a dating app. I snickered to myself as I did the same thing with the Ally, only we didn't even make it to the exclusive conversation. We still talk and text, but it's just not the same. He said he was looking for stimulation. I worry he got that and now he's done. But for me, I'm over here all overstimulated and intense for him. I'm textbook what not to do.

December

Wednesday, December 1

I texted DMV guy. He wrote back immediately. He then sent a strange Snoopy gif that said, "Happy December 1st," and Snoopy was dancing with Woodstock (the yellow bird friend?). It was like something a grandparent would send to their grandchild. It did not make my lady bits perk up. I decided to give it a shot and agree to dinner. We're going next week to a local spot.

Friday, December 3

The Ally is talking about a trip here for a day. He has other business in the city so it's not just to see me. I worry about seeing him again as I know I'll get even further into my feels. We have this cat and mouse thing going. I say or push too much, he pulls back. I feel like shit for being all feely and back off. He then gets all dreamy and sweet again, and I'm pulled right back to feelings I can't control. This is why I didn't want a long-distance thing. I'm not good at this.

Saturday, December 4

I went out with DMV guy. My dating experience is limited, but I can unequivocally say this was the worst date I've ever been on. He didn't look the same as I remembered, although at the DMV he had a winter hat, coat, and mask on. I didn't realize he was a solid ten years older than me. He also started off dinner with a prayer. It was sweet when he held my hand to pray, but it felt off. Like he was trying too hard. I did not feel a spark and said so after, but he's sent a million texts since then with different links to properties he's investing in (he's an investment banker) and I just don't care at all. Money doesn't perk up my lady bits, my dude. I have my own.

Friday, December 10

The Ally was here, just for the night. I only got to spend a few hours with him. He was short on time, so I met him at his hotel with my favorite meatballs. He liked the fact I brought him food. I just wanted him. All of him. His face, his brain, his silly impressions. He's genius-level smart. As a fortysomething black man, he has such a different experience from mine. He helps me see things about myself that I'm not aware of. I don't ever get bored listening to him talk. He talks a lot. Tells lots of funny stories; his experiences as a black man which I love hearing. I find myself waiting for his next word. I've never felt like this about a man. But he's going to leave, not commit to anything or give any indication of what we are, and then I'm going to be alone in my feels again. I don't like the aftermath of my Ally visits.

Thursday, December 16

My girl Iris has found me a place. It's a three-bedroom high-rise with a northeast corner view a few blocks from the town house. I'm so excited to check it out. Iris has blown me away as a realtor and friend. She put a sign up in her building looking for three bedrooms, and somebody contacted her. A woman named Catherine. I'm going to view Catherine's unit later this week. Oh, I hope this works out. I love the high-rise I'm in now, but two bedrooms with three kids is absurd. We can't keep living like this.

Wednesday, December 22

I am overwhelmed. I'm taking my kids on my first solo vacation. We're going to Florida after Christmas. Sister is meeting us there with her husband and kids. I'm scared to fly and do all the things solo with the kids, but I know I can do it.

I saw Catherine's unit and immediately fell in love. She's a mosaic tile artist and hand tiled a column in the living room with colors from the lake and waves. I adored her as a human too. I love creative types. I'm a lefty and have love for creative-leaning brains. I'm going to put in an offer. So stressful. Can I afford this? All the mortgage people are saying yes, but it's hard not to think of all the what-ifs.

Saturday, December 25

I got the apartment! My dream home. Iris was instrumental in making it happen. She lives in the building too and will be a few floors away from me. I'm excited!

I'm taking the girls to Florida tomorrow on vacation. I'm trying to pack them now, and I'm anxious about forgetting things.

Tuesday, December 28

We made it to sunny Florida. The girls are happy playing with their cousins. OMG, the plane ride with three kids solo. I'm used to zone defense where KD would take one, and I'd have the other two in a row. We'd work together to keep them occupied, but doing it solo was hard as hell. The youngest can walk (she's fucking six) but gets whiny after a few minutes in the airport and wants me to carry her. The oldest is helpful but gets lost in gazing at the world around her (totally gets this from me). My middle girl is usually well behaved, but she's picky AF, so finding her things to eat or places that have chicken nuggets at all hours is not easy. BUT we made it to Florida, yay!

I'm getting copious amounts of gossip and life upheaval talk time with sister. Her in-laws are staying in the Airbnb we're in. I gotta say, I don't miss vacations with my former in-laws. Mine were on my honeymoon. What a bad omen.

Friday, December 31

We went to a New Year's Eve party at the hotel. The kids played on the beach. We had a nice time, but I can't help but feel unsettled. I have the Ally on the brain. I drink too much with sister. I call Ally after too much vodka. I tell him I love him. I immediately regret being that vulnerable. I'm putting too much on him. My feelings are all over the place and spilling on him. I am 100 percent what not to do in a relationship and I don't even have a relationship with him. I barely have a situationship. Clean up on aisle 5.

January

Saturday, January 1

I hate waking up after doing something drunk the night before and feeling cringe. While I do love him, I should not have said that to Ally. I don't know where I stand with him or what we are, if it's going anywhere; and for me, the not knowing part makes me irrational. I want reassurance I'm not alone feeling this way, and if he's not feeling it, let me move on with my life.

Feeling like a giant failure today. Big ol' pity party for myself. I failed in marriage. I failed to have the feelings a wife should have for her husband. I have those feelings, *literally all the feelings,* for the Ally—a man who can't give me reassurance that whatever we are is progressing into something. He's just so casual. He'll say he has love for me and he still reaches out every few days. It might be easiest just to cut ties completely, but that makes me feel incredibly sad.

At one point I told him someone had flirted with me while I was out and about. I was sharing it as it was—something that happened that day and it brightened my spirits. He said that was triangulation. I hadn't heard the word before. Apparently, a tactic people use to get others to do something or feel a type of way? Had to look it up. The interwebs tell me this:

> What does it mean to triangulate a person?
>
> Triangulation happens **when one or both of the people involved in the conflict try to pull a third person into the dynamic**, often with the goal of: deflecting some of the tension. creating another conflict to take the spotlight off the original issue. reinforcing their sense of rightness or superiority. Feb 25, 2021

In reading that definition I'm not even sure what flirting has to do with any of it. The Ally's point was mentioning someone else was intentional to make him feel a type of way, maybe that was my intent? I don't know anymore.

I do not share things like this to hurt him, but I do want to know if we're just a casual thing, and if so, is he dating others, and if so, I should be too, right? But I'm not. I'm tying myself up in knots for someone unavailable, and I just want to know if unavailable is how it'll always be.

Sunday, January 2

Flying back from Florida with the kids was one of the top five worst experiences of my life. KD always booked our travel. He was so good at finding the right hotels or AirBnb spots, getting airfare, and price checking—stuff I am terrible at. In my haste with booking the four airplane tickets, I thought I'd booked a 7:55 a.m. return flight but it was 7:55 p.m. We didn't get home until after midnight, and kids have school tomorrow.

I had a lot of plane time to think. Of course, all I think about is the Ally. I am incredibly sad and confused. Mad at myself for falling for someone so unavailable. I want to stop talking to him and run away so this feeling goes away, but I care about him. I know he cares for me. He's going through hell right now with work, his own life, and ex, kids, and all the things. I also just got divorced, and he's been burned before. He has patience and thoughtful insight about so many things, so why can't I just go with the flow?

Wednesday, January 5

I've scared Ally. He doesn't know what to do with me coming at him with all my feelings—anger at not getting reassurance but also love. So much damn love. And he said he's got love for me too. He didn't say he loved me, though. He is very careful with his words. I love and hate this at the same time.

He tells me he wants to feel safe. I worry that my up and down moods are showing how unsafe I am. I'm like a damn bomb. The instability and inconsistency are wearing on me, though. He called every day early on and said things like "long distance means trips to California" when convincing me to give him a shot. The daily calls are gone. He doesn't mention or invite me to California. I go back to what he said he originally wanted: stimulation. I'm tired of being stimulation.

Tuesday, January 11

I'm closing on the dream home at the end of this month. It's keeping me busy and my mind off Ally. I need to schedule movers and do all the things. Buy beds and mattresses, dressers, and dishes. KD has been helpful and is always willing to have me take things from the town house. He's been a remarkable co-parent and friend through it all.

Friday, January 14

Packing, all the packing. I keep meaning to get movers, and then every day I convince myself I can do it solo. I don't have that much stuff. I have the boxes and the closets done. I think it'll be okay if I just rent a truck or a big van. Oy, this should be interesting.

Saturday, January 22

I was incredibly stressed today. I don't have the girls so I'm packing like crazy so I'm ready to move next week. The beds I ordered are all being delivered on different dates and times. The couch I ordered is huge, and I hope it fits. I do not measure, not with furniture, recipes, or really anything.

When I don't have the girls, I usually have a plan so I'm not left to dwell on whatever I'm mopey about. Today's plan was to pack and get things in order. I also stripped the beds, washed the sheets, and just generally got the apartment pulled together. I have two vibrators so, of course, charging those while the girls were away topped my list.

In one of my more embarrassing moments, the maintenance guy popped by to fix the furnace. I did not know he was coming over or that the furnace had an issue. He had to step over the two vibrators charging to get to the furnace. I tried to kick them under the bed, but he'd already seen them and the damage was done. As he was leaving, he gave me a double thumbs up, and I'll never not cringe when I think about this.

Monday, January 24

MOVING DAY. We had a few hiccups, but in the end, I got my dream home. What a moment. I own two homes now! I built this life. Incredible for a small-town Indiana girl.

Iris went so far above and beyond for me. She fought for the right parking spots and guided me through the whole process. I will never let that girl out of my life.

I rented a cargo van. I had no idea what a cargo van was but it sounded legit. Does it have pockets like cargo pants? I picked it up on the south side and it's huge. A giant van/truck/machine with a cage in the back. The girls are in heaven. I go to a McDonald's drive-through and they're just free ranging in the cage in the back of the van (we are driving in the city very slowly—seatbelts weren't available in the cage). The van is too high to clear the McDonald's drive-through, so I have to back out and actually go in the place. I get the Happy Meals and toss them in the cage. Peak mom effort today.

The window washers are outside of the high-rise as I'm packing up the last of my things. I see maintenance guy who apparently doubles as a window washer. He sees me and with dead-ass eye contact gives me two thumbs up AGAIN. I guarantee this guy has told everyone this tale. The thirsty divorcee double vibrator lady upstairs. I wonder what the doormen think. Old man Frank probably intrigued or horrified. I'm not sure. OMG, I am so glad I'm moving.

February

Wednesday, February 2

We made it through the move. The apartment is everything I wanted. The girls are so excited too.

I hurt my arm. Like an idiot, I was carrying two Rubbermaid bins up the stairs. I was rushing to get my middle kid's room ready. My eldest's room was done and I had visions of my middle girl being upset her room wasn't done. I had to hurry to get it all done by 3:15 p.m. when school let out.

I stumbled down two stairs and scraped my arm on a cement post. I've broken both arms before so I'm no stranger to pain, but this hurt like a bitch. I cleaned up the blood, put a giant Band-aid on it, and kept working. Middle came home from school and loved her room. Nobody noticed I was wincing in pain.

Friday, February 4

My arm is bandaged up. It is red hot to the touch. I keep Neosporin on it at all times. Urgent care says it is not broken, thankfully.

The girls are settling in. I have a three-bedroom. I had a vision of the middle and youngest sharing a room. So far, the youngest has been sleeping in my room. Middle often sleeps with me too. I have shared a bed with one of my girls for the last twelve years. It all started when they were babies. I couldn't do cry it out (where you let a baby cry and teach them to self-soothe—the sleep training approach). I always picked up my girls and held them or nursed them to get them back to sleep. Here I am so many years later and I still love snuggling up with my girls when they are asleep. I look at their little faces, hands, and feet; their bodies breathing. I feel calm and peaceful when I'm next to them. It feels so right to sleep with them, but I worry I've done the wrong thing, and they'll never be able to sleep alone. My oldest is pretty good about sleeping in her own bed, though, so I have hope. But, fuck, she's almost a teenager now.

I always wanted to sleep with my girls, but not with KD. I have guilt about that. I put a wedge between us with motherhood, while he put a wedge between us with words and work. I couldn't let the girls cry. I'm so negative on myself about this.

Monday, February 7

I have food poisoning. I got pita bread and hummus yesterday. I was vomiting all night. I'm still shaking today. I can't keep food down. My head is pounding. I'm living out of boxes and have no energy to move.

Wednesday, February 9

I have thrown up more in the past few days than I ever have in my life. That's including having hyperemesis with my pregnancies and having to take Zofran to keep food down well beyond the first trimester. Oof, I am sick. Back to urgent care. The doctor said there's been a listeria outbreak at this restaurant (where I had hummus), and I just need to let it run its course. He laughs that he just saw me a few weeks ago for my arm. Never does he connect the two incidents, though.

Tuesday, February 15

Forty-five. Such a significant number for me today. It is my forty-fifth birthday.

Turns out, I didn't have food poisoning. Well, I did, but I also had an active infection in my arm from moving a few weeks ago. Food poisoning + gnarly arm infection pushed my body into sepsis. Too many bacteria in my bloodstream and my body couldn't fight anymore. I was in full-blown septic shock, with organs failing by the time I got to the ER. The doctors gave me a spinal tap to check for meningitis, an ultrasound, and a host of other things. I'm so grateful they were able to save my life.

In the days that followed in a hospital bed I was grateful to be alive but also angry with myself. Angry that I missed this and I didn't go to the ER sooner. I kept listening to an urgent care doctor when I should have listened to my own intuition. This wasn't just food poisoning.

I had to stay in the hospital for a few days. I could see messages and calls coming in like crazy. A few weeks ago, my boss told me they were promoting me to a US role and now they had announced it publicly. I was so excited. It was nice gratification after taking such a risky move in my career—my first year at the new gig was paying off. I was beaming with pride but also in a ridiculous amount of pain.

All of my friends were texting too. So many 'What can I do to help?' messages. Everyone wants to help, which is so lovely, but I'm too sick to respond.

Friday, February 18

The picture above popped up in my memories from February 2013. Eight years ago. I remember where I was when I took it. Cold Wed in Chicago, left work (an actual office), sun was still out, and I remember feeling disconnected. I saw this "Love" sign and thought it was interesting but cheesy. Like, we're *all fine*. Don't need more litter on Chicago streets. I took a picture and posted a sort of snarky, guess this dumb "love" thing is getting handed out blah blah comment, thinking my parents would laugh.

Eight years later, looking at my post, knowing what I know now and seeing how the world has changed, I am especially reflective. No matter what your family looks like, the pandemic, and the real, raw issues and pain humans are dealing with every day while being good employees and doing all the self-care are mind-blowingly different now. Now we need all the love we can get.

While we have a million daily stressors and new ways to live and work to figure out, we must be vigilant about our own care. I should have paid attention to my own health.

Saturday, February 19

I am in all my feels. I could have died. I could have left my girls without a mother. I need to pay attention but also not be so hard on myself, but I AM.

I realized I have this pattern in my life, and as I've said it aloud to friends and family, it appears many people do this. The pattern goes like this: I take on too much, I make a snap decision under stress, and hurt myself in irreversible ways. This sepsis episode is no different.

I hurt my arm carrying two Rubbermaid bins upstairs so I could get my middle kid's room ready in my new apartment, as my eldest's room was ready and I didn't want to let my middle girl down. I was hurrying. I had to get it done before school was over at 3:15 p.m. Without skipping a beat, I kept going after that injury. A few days later, food poisoning struck. Those two things together were almost lethal all because I was hurrying to get a room put together for validation and a pat on the back that 'I'm a good mom.' I get choked up now thinking about that. My middle kid is the chillest of the bunch too. She likely wouldn't care but, somehow, I cared so much I was careless about my own health. This revelation shakes me to my core. I am not a machine. I need care and attention, just like my daughters do.

I am not invincible. There will always be things that knock you out for a week, two, maybe more—a health scare, caring for family member, etc. I know when it happens to me again I will be ready.

Tuesday, February 22

I am so lucky to be alive. I am grateful and have boundless energy right now. I want to tell all the moms, employees, and friends I know to slow the fuck down and take care of themselves.

Do you remember those gas station change boxes where you could take a penny if you needed one or give a penny if you had one? They were everywhere but also nowhere. I don't remember ever taking a penny. "Pffft. A penny? Not going to help, anyway," so just *keep moving*.

I suggest we all reframe—take the penny next time. The penny is a promise of help when you need it most no matter how small. I'm using this "take a penny" mantra with my teams at work. Like the kids say, it's a whole vibe.

The pandemic created a whole new style of hybrid remote work. None of us, not even the fortysomething boss lady making magic every day, has a clue if we're doing it 'right.' There is no test to study for. We are the test. We check off that to-do list and add to it every day, but what's it all for?

You won't get it all done. I look at this penny visual as asking, *REALLY asking for, and receiving* help. I use it daily now. Take the penny. Every single day. Take five.

My new thing is connecting with people. Offering real help. People all around are willing to help, but our remote world (and pride of this Gen X silent sufferer) turned us into machines that get it all done (yay!) but to our own demise (boo!). I'm going to change that one person at a time.

Friday, February 25

The Ally was in town for a brief stop. I saw him for a few hours. It was off. I was off. My mind was all over the place, and I was still reeling from almost dying. He asked me how high my fever was when I went to the hospital, and he mentioned black men in his rural hometown losing limbs to diabetes and dying every day. I took it as he was inferring I wasn't all that sick, or perhaps I should look on the bright side? I'm not sure. He likely wasn't inferring that, and I was too sick to think straight.

I've been on brain swelling reduction meds since I was discharged from the hospital. My mind is oatmeal. The visit did not go well, but I'm also taking stock of my whole life right now. I've been talking to Ally for months and we're nowhere close to official anything. I've never seen his home nor been invited. Perhaps this needed to happen so I can move on.

Monday, February 28

While things with the Ally are on ice, I'm making an impact every single day.

I remember lying in my hospital bed, looking at my work email and Teams IMs. It all seemed so pointless. I thought about the countless meetings, summits, conferences, webinars, and whatever other word corporate people come up with for 'time wasted.' While there are valuable meetings, overall, I had been spreading myself too thin and not paying attention to the important stuff. I had been dusting the coffee table (going to pointless meetings) when the house was on fire (my body).

After getting sick, I see now how little I was doing every day that made an impact. I oversee a team of people and we're doing great work, but I'm on autopilot.

One of my strengths is my ability to connect with humans. I make a difference one-on-one with people. This is where I shine. One relationship, one person, one client at a time. I have been living each day with intention since I got sick. I hope I don't lose this mentality. Being thoughtful with how I approach my day, what meetings I join, who I interact with, and where I put my energy, it all matters immensely.

I'm also doing this in my personal life. I'm checking in on my village. Real calls where I listen to their voice, hear what is in their heart, and connect. Solving problems together, be it at home, at the kids' school, or with friends at happy hour.

March

Thursday, March 3

One of the bigger things coming out of my health scare was my lack of preparation. I had friends, family, and colleagues texting things like "I heard you're in the hospital! What can I do to help?" Everyone wanted to help, but I was too sick to respond to all the pings. And I'm single so I have no deputy.

We should be trading a Google doc with rows for our village, and each of us shares the random, weird things you'd need should you go down and be unreachably ill for days or longer—the "penny" you might need. Fill up your tab so your pennies are identified and known—my middle kid only eats spaghetti, chicken nuggets, and frozen broccoli so, hey, village, let's meal train that. I pair my health scares and dream job promotions with Raisinets in a resealable bag so add that too!

Get really specific on what help looks like to you because when that health scare happens (when! It ALWAYS happens at some point) you have identified the "pennies" that would help. In a moment's notice your village is activated. Our current system is: we get sick, friends and colleagues want to help, and reach out, asking, "How can I help?"[3] but you're so ill you can't respond so nobody knows how to help, and a few people do a meal train, where everything piles up and food is wasted. Then everyone goes back to their own lives.

I still have sixty-plus unread texts, all lovely, and I want to help them help me because I know that's what they want to do. And we'd all be better for it.

Saturday, March 5

Ally. The one person I wish I could connect with, and we aren't connected at all.

We still talk but it's not the same. I asked him what he wants. He says he wants to understand me and to feel safe. I try to do this, but it's been months and I still don't know if this will ever be a real thing and I so desperately want it to be. I want him to say, "We're committed to each other" or "I want you to come to California to see my life"—really, anything that tells me I mean as much to him as he does to me. That I'm not out on this tree branch all vulnerable alone.

He tells me I need to be divorced longer and take more time before a relationship. I disagree. I have never been so clear in my life. He struggles with his own mental health and had an awful divorce. I feel like he projects his situation onto me. I don't have the same situation. KD and I are friends. KD comes over to fix drawers off the hook

---

[3] Come over and pet my fat cat in the sun, please, one hour minimum, keys at front desk.

in the kids' bathroom at my new apartment. The Ally doesn't even speak to the mother of his kids. Completely different situations.

The Ally has been hurt before—actually, "eviscerated" is the word he used—by people who claimed to care about him, but when they got hurt or disappointed by something he did, they lashed out at him. I am not this, but he's only known me for a few months so I understand the pause.

He does hurt me by keeping me at arm's length. His inconsistency upsets me the most. He was so strong out of the gate and says he feels the same, but where did that guy go? The one that would call every day and make me laugh, and we'd talk about the mundane of life. Now I'm lucky if he reaches out once a week. The inconsistency has been jarring.

He has a big job too and lots of investors asking, "What have you done for me lately?" Stress and pressure everywhere. He tells me he's not in the right place for a relationship. I respect and understand that, but what is this then? A situationship 'til the end of time? I don't want that nor do I have time for it.

Even without Ally, I'll be okay. I'm on such a high changing lives that I'm starting not to care as much. This feels like me.

Wednesday, March 9

I'm a tallish and skinny woman. I didn't have weight to lose when I got sick. I had already lost weight from the stress of divorce, but the sepsis scare hit me much harder. The fatigue, brain fog from my organs being infiltrated by bacteria, and the fallout from all the medication they had to give me. I do not feel like myself.

I've been going to follow-up doctor appointments and doing bloodwork. While I only lost five pounds, it's noticeable on my 5'8" frame—reminds me of being called Skeletor when I was in high school.[4]

My doctor thinks I may need to have my gallbladder removed. It was just too far gone with sepsis ("severe right quadrant"—they said this over and over when I was in and out of consciousness at the ER which means my right kidney, gallbladder, top part of my liver, and such), but I'm hopeful I can reverse it. The mental damage will take some time to fix, but physical damage and digestive health, I'm hopeful I can fix them quicker. I have a food background and my master's degree is in human nutrition so I feel up for the challenge. Operation *Robo Cop save gallbladder!*

Friday, March 11

I've been reading everything I can on gallbladder restoration. I'm calling it restoration as I like visuals. The gallbladder stores bile; bile helps break down fat. So, my visual is making my bile storage facility the prettiest on the block with healthy foods (fiber, fruits, and vegetables, a ton of water too).

My labs are improving. I'm a modern marvel to my doctor.

---

[4] Damn kids were mean. I was also called Robo Cop as a freshman when I broke my arm and had a metal rod in it. Wonder why my self-esteem wasn't great. Grew up with "quit your crying" type parenting and horrific insults from classmates that hit on my biggest insecurities.

Tuesday, March 15

The Ally reached out. He wants to see me on April 1. Actual time together so we can talk. He's been under so much stress at work and our last visit was not good. My brain fog is improving. His guard was up, though, and he seemed down.

Thursday, March 17

St. Patrick's Day in your twenties was fun. You'd go out, hit some bars, wear green, drink your face off.

St. Patrick's Day married was fun too. Hanging out at friends' homes and having a boozy St. Patrick's Day breakfast/brunch with kids running around so it resembled a playdate, but was actually a mini rager with kids (and, man, did the parents need this day).

St. Patrick's Day divorced is insanely fun. I do shamrock crafts with the girls, and we use more glitter than I anticipated, but as I tell my girls, "a mess means we had fun." I also love that I don't need to drink alcohol to have fun. I drank a lot while I was married; never as much as KD, but definitely more than I do now. I don't ever feel like I need to share wine at dinner with KD or be pressured to have alcohol at a restaurant on a date night or whatever. I can just be me and she's ready to give alcohol up entirely.

Saturday, March 19

I've gained muscle mass back! My liver and gallbladder function are almost back to normal. I am so proud of myself. It's nuts when something life-threatening happens to you. At first, everyone cared, but a week or so later, my parents and family were back to giving me shit and cracking jokes in the family group text.

→ Me, still vomiting and nauseous almost daily a month out of hospital and telling my family.

My mom (no master's degree in human nutrition and dietetics): You don't need a gallbladder, who cares?

Me (has a master's degree in human nutrition and dietetics): Um, I care.

I've gone through so much therapy over the years. This moment in my life is an example of how I put all the therapy into practice. My self-esteem comes from me. I do not need validation from anyone else. I am enough. So when my mom rags on me and doesn't give me any credit as her daughter who got a 4.0 in nutrition school (that I paid for) by dismissing any consideration or care I have of my own gallbladder, I do not feel less than or that I'm not enough. I know I'm enough. I bat her passive-aggressive (and often aggressive-aggressive digs—she called me a dipshit in front of my daughters recently) away, and it does not affect me anymore. I have no expectations of her, so I am no longer disappointed by anything.

Wednesday, March 23

One of my best mom friends, Mary, is turning fifty! Hard to believe we're all getting there. We're headed to Vegas in a few weeks. I'm horrified at the group text. The bodycon dresses? The strappy shoes?

The sequins? I'm in bed at 9:00 p.m. and strappy shoes make me crappy to be around.

They are all so jealous I can make out with abandon. I can't imagine doing this but, meh, why not?

Tuesday, March 29

While figuring out my bodycon situation for Vegas packing, I'm also talking to the Ally more. He seems stressed. He is still coming on April 1. I'm trying to make it all less heavy. Last time it was heavy. I know I just wanted reassurance that we were something and he couldn't give it (and likely very thoughtfully said why) and I got hurt. I don't remember all the particulars—seriously, those brain swelling reduction meds made me crazy—but I do feel bad for lashing out at a human I care about because he was telling me no. He wasn't even telling me no, he was telling me, "I'm here now. I like you, but not yet." And I couldn't deal with that.

April

Monday, April 1

The Ally was supposed to come today. He cancelled. He's been having mental health struggles while running a big start-up. The pressure is getting to him. He needs to take care of himself so he can be there for his kids. I understand this and truly want him to be better. I'm worried about this man. I tell him I'll support him and anything he needs—all the dumb things people say. I send my last message and I don't know what to do next. Just leave him alone while he sorts this? Wish I didn't care so much.

Wednesday, April 3

The Vegas mom group chat has been going on for at least a year. This fiftieth birthday trip has been postponed with the pandemic and managing everyone's already maxed schedules. Now the text is blowing up every three minutes with mom excitement. These moms really need this. They're all going tomorrow, but I only do two nights in Vegas so I'm not headed there until early Friday morning. I wish them well with night 1 sequins.

Friday, April 5

My first *sort of* vacation single. It's Vegas, so not the first spot I'd pick, but I packed a yellow bikini and I know I'm going to laugh my ass off. I met my posse at the hotel. We have two rooms of four moms each.

I get to the hotel room, and two are sleeping, and Mary is up in workout clothes ready for the gym. I say fuck it, I've been up since 5:00 a.m., why not work out now in Vegas? So we hit the gym. Mary is fifty years old. She was up until at least 1:00 a.m. doing dinner, casino, club, wine, wine, more wine, and here she is running 9.0 on a treadmill at 8:30 a.m. the morning after.

I send the Ally a witty text. Just keeping things light, knowing all the stuff he's got happening. He always opens my eyes to my whiteness. Immediately he says that's some white girl shit, working out in the morning after partying all night. Is it? I had no idea but I'm 100 percent guilty of this behavior. Gets the toxins out or something?

Saturday, April 6

Vegas. It has been the best of times. It has been the worst of times.

I love one-on-one time with my mom friends. We all have daily struggles and moments of brain damage one moment at a time over the course of our children's formative years while we're trying to just BE ourselves (the woman you were before the tiny humans you created).

I've spent all day with these women. We rarely get interrupted talk time like this as we're always dripping with kids asking for things. While the setting around us (disgusting pool party with cloudy—likely jizz—water and live DJ) could have been better, the conversation and listening I did today warmed my heart. I needed this. I laughed until my stomach hurt. I have been so lucky to fall into this group of women all connected to the lovely Catholic school where we started the girls in preschool ages ago.

But it was also the worst of times.

The ladies love these greasy LAPD guys in the cabana next to us. They are wearing wristbands, and I swear they show up everywhere, in every location where we are, and I don't understand how it's happening. I'm the only single one so I'm used as the icebreaker—"Here! She's single!" Pretty sure ladies just want to use me to start flirting themselves, but I roll with it. The cops are disgusting, though. Off the bat, the first asks why my husband left me.

I have heard this a few times since I got divorced. There is no good answer here. Push for accuracy that I left? But we both realized it and are co-parenting nicely and, really, nobody wins no matter how you phrase the question. Like some greasy dude in Vegas cares about all that, but the mere inference I was left irritates me.

I'm underwhelmed by the men around me. I have my children. I make dope cash. I do not need a man for shit at this point in my life, so, you, Mr. Random Police Guy claiming, "I'm only married when I'm in LA, not in Vegas" can fuck right off.

I'm in bed by 10:00 p.m. But let me tell you about the after-pool party. Sushi! We were wearing tight, too small, too short dresses with strappy, painful clickity clack heels, and we were TIRED. And grumpy. And cold. We'd been drinking for hours all day. Our Vegas outfits were sexy as hell, but all of that strappy shit offers no real air cover, and the AC in Vegas is set on Arendelle ice when Elsa loses her shit.

We walk to the restaurant through old casinos, hotels, or just ugly carpet with weird-smelling air in tunnels, and I have no idea where we are—underground Vegas tunnels of pain (the fucking strappy shoes!) or shame? Finally make it to the sushi restaurant. Eating takes hours. I'm falling asleep. Moms are trying to rally. They want to gamble for a bit and hit some clubs. My feet are screaming at me and it's only 9:00 p.m. How did I do this in my twenties?

I limp out of the restaurant, pretend to gamble for three minutes, and duck behind a slot machine to run to the room. I'm queen of the fade, Irish goodbye, or whatever you want to call it. My mom knows this. I'm in bed eating room-service molten lava chocolate cake by 9:45 p.m. My flight is early. I feel responsible.

Wake up at 4:00 a.m. Moms are still not back in the room. The fuck?

Heading to the airport at 6:30 a.m. Moms run in, pack bags, and we quickly head to airport. These fifty-year-olds stayed up all night clubbing. I am just in awe. These women are fucking G R O W N. I am proud.

Tuesday, April 12

Our community is broken.

Mary, our fiftieth birthday Vegas celebratee, has just lost her husband. The father of her children. He killed himself.

Her daughter called me from the parking lot of where it happened. She's friends with my daughter.

I dropped to my knees. The wind knocked out of me. I tried to be calm for her daughter. She needs me.

And Mary. My dear friend Mary. The heart of our school community. She knows everyone. She's involved in all the committees, she is a badass executive and manages a social calendar Paris Hilton would envy (I'm old and don't have any newer socialite references), and she is a mom. She is a good mom. Immediately, all of us moms are there for her.

Last time a few of us saw each other we were laughing at sunrise in a Vegas hotel room, scrambling to pack our shit to get to our flight. And a few days later, we're around a kitchen island in Mary's house. All of us crying, reeling, and unable to process. The food and more food continue to arrive. It is stacking up on every counter and in every part of the fridge and freezer. My anxiety, sadness, and utter shock make it hard to keep speaking. Mary is stoic. She is calm. She is tired. My heart breaks for her. And her babies. Her husband's parents and sisters. We will never be the same.

Wednesday, April 13

This doesn't make sense for our school community. Mary's husband was an incredible human. Everyone was dumbfounded. How could this happen?

Mary's love story was very yin and yang. Mary is type A, driven, and her husband was laidback, genius-level smart, and incredibly funny.

This world was a lot for her husband, though. He struggled with mental health, and many did not know this. I had a special bond with him as we shared a similar inappropriate sense of humor. I was broken, but my eyes were on Mary. I watched her face, just waiting for her to break down. It had to be coming. She can't keep going at this pace. The visitors. Nonstop. The food and stress, calls, texts, and gifts and deliveries. I don't know how she is doing it all. I am in awe of her.

Friday, April 15

We're all in a state of shock. I check in on Mary daily after school drop-off. I've had important people in my life die, but not like this. It's so raw. My heart hurts for her children and for Mary. Every day, so stoic and moving through the giant to-do list.

With every crisis, at first, everyone is all-in and all around you. Over time, they get back to their own lives and you're just a downer. They say tropey things like "I'm praying for you," but does any of that help? Or that "God took him for a reason" or whatever bullshit people come up with. I just watch Mary's face, listen to her voice, and try to be there in whatever way she needs.

Mary's daughter had a fever, and the school called to say she needed to be picked up. Mary was unable to get her, so I grabbed her. I got some one-on-one time with her. We painted. She made a beautiful sky with clouds and a rainbow of colors. She said it was her dad looking down from heaven. I could feel my eyes welling up. It is so hard to be strong for others when you need a hug too.

Tuesday, April 19

I called KD when I heard the news about Mary's husband. I wanted him to know immediately, as Mary's daughter is close with my oldest and they talk often. It was hard to share emotional news and not lean on him like a husband. He's been such a rock for all of us. While we didn't work married, we work well as friends and parents. I'm proud of that. It's been a long year. It's still awkward here and there, and I'm sure it will be for years to come. I see joy on his face, and he laughs more. He's happier this way, and I knew he would be.

I'm happier too, but I often feel unsettled. All the therapy in the world won't change that. I get shit done. If there's something in my life that feels incomplete, I want to complete it. And right now I'm not used to life on my own. I'm learning all of it but, of course, I want to learn it all faster to feel more settled. Since my health scare, I've slowed down considerably. I take pride in how far I've come and all I'm doing on my own. I'm a positive example of hard work and living your truth. My daughters see that every day, and it makes me proud.

Thursday, April 21

The Ally hasn't been there for me as he's got his own world of problems. I called him, and he said it was triggering to hear about suicide as he's been personally impacted by it in the past.

He's still back home dealing with his own mental health. I care for him deeply. He went from calling me all the time, constant messages and chats, to barely reaching out every few days. It hurts, but I also know it's not about me. He has his own path and his own mind. He opened my eyes to a world I've imagined but never acted on. He's not capable of giving any more than that, and I need to accept it. Sometimesy—this is only word I can come up with for his behavior.

Sunday, May 1

I remember listening to Alicia Keys's "Girl on Fire" at the gym years ago. It's such a powerful song. Years ago, when I listened to it, I felt stagnant. I didn't feel on fire. Now listening to it after getting an incredible new job, moving twice, getting divorced, buying my dream home, raising our girls, and surviving septic shock, I feel powerful. I've come so far.

I got both feet on the ground and I'm burning it down. I changed my life in a year. I still have so much to do. My girls are doing fine, KD is happier than he's ever been, and I'm wondering what I'm going to fix next.

+++

Epilogue

Out of all my fortysomething years, this one has been the most transformative.

Messy, unsettling, sick, and painful. But also joyful, resilient, and excited for the future, knowing I'm living my truth now. Alone without a man beside me but surrounded by my girls, a lovely friendship with KD, and family and friends who continue to support us.

I'm calling this first year of transformation my year of getting undiddy with it. All the undid my youngest talked about, not just the disabled iPad or the egg toy, but a life built over many decades that didn't feel quite right—parts that needed to be undone and reworked. I did it one day at a time, one "thing" at a time. Here's what I learned:

Getting undiddy with it

1. **The unsettled, misaligned feeling won't go away.** It won't fix itself. For me, it took a bold move—changing jobs after being with the same company for more than twenty years. I was too scared to leave, too smart to stay. Leaving was one

of the best things I ever did. The new position gave me more motivation to align myself with who I really am. I knew I was capable of more. I knew I could be challenged and might even be happier, but complacency and comfort crept in. I was a mom, three daughters, a marriage that wasn't great, the house payments, the bills, the family drama. It's often easier to do nothing. Going after a bigger job and not only getting it with a fat pay raise but also immediately doing well in the role gave me the confidence to do even more hard things. It was like jumping out of a plane and it sparked big movements elsewhere in my life. Now I look for big moves. They are catalysts. If you're feeling stuck, **make a big move,** be it a career change, different job, moving to a new city, going back to school, learning a new skill, or whatever it is that your mind drifts to when you get that gnawing unsettled feeling. Take the first step.

2. **Make yourself a priority.** Easier said than done, right? It took almost dying for me to realize I need to care for myself the same way I care for my daughters. I'm the same little girl inside and she needs love, hugs, cuddles, and reassurance too. I did a ton of work to understand myself and my past, how it impacted my marriage, and how I can unlearn negative behavior patterns I've had since childhood. That "I'm not good enough" feeling. I love myself. I love the body I'm in. I even love my sexy bits. Therapy, especially different types, kept me sane and helped me stop being so hard on myself. I can feed myself all the healthy food in the world, work out six days a week, yet still talk to myself inside my brain like I'm a big piece of shit, and that was the crux of my problem. Negative thinking and not feeling good enough. Get in

therapy—remote, in-person, podcasts, or whatever form you gravitate toward. Therapy evolves to meet you where you are now. For me, visualization exercises and redirection helped the most. I also remind myself constantly that thoughts aren't facts.

3. **Slow down.** Too often we're on autopilot. We go through the motions of our day. The job, the kids, the work events. We aren't present for most of it. After my hospital scare, I made the most of each day by focusing on individuals and building on those relationships. I was in a big ol' hurry to do divorce correctly; to somehow get an A+ in it, but that's not possible. There isn't some arbitrary finish line, be it marriage in your twenties or completing divorce like acing the driver's test. The only finish line is death. Slowing down and being more thoughtful in my day-to-day interactions have changed my life.

4. **Love takes many forms.** KD and I lost romantic love many years ago, but our friendship and genuine care for one another and the family we created will never stop. I know romantic love is out there for me somewhere. When it's right, I'll know. For now, my girls, my sister, and my friends and family are my true loves, especially sister. We are twins, and twin sister love is different from anything. Seeing her dig deep to be there for me at my worst this year (every single day) has given me a whole new appreciation for her and what she means to me. If nothing else, we'll have such a fun retirement together! Plus, we still have so many things to do.

+++